Lifeblood

In 2006, Wall Street wizard and philanthropist Ray Chambers flicked through some holiday snapshots taken by his friend, development economist Jeffrey Sachs, and remarked on the placid beauty of a group of sleeping Malawian children.

"They're not sleeping," Sachs told Chambers. "They're in malarious comas." A few days later, they were all dead.

So begins Chambers's race to eradicate a disease that has haunted humankind since Hippocrates, still infects half a billion people a year, and kills a million of them. The campaign draws in presidents, celebrities, scientists, and billions of dollars and becomes a stunning success, saving millions of lives and propelling Africa toward prosperity. By drawing heavily on business, Chambers also reinvents foreign aid, showing how helping can be both efficient and in all our interests.

As he follows two years of the campaign, award-winning journalist Alex Perry takes the reader across the globe, from a terrifying visit to the most malarious town on earth to the White House, from the forests of the Democratic Republic of Congo to soccer's World Cup. In *Lifeblood*, Perry weaves together science and history with on-the-ground reporting and a searing exposé of aid as he documents Chambers's frenetic campaign. The result is an incisive and often surprising portrait of modern Africa, a story of revolution in aid and development, and a thrilling and all-too-rare tale of humanitarian triumph, with profound implications for how to build a better world.

Lifeblood

How to Change the World
One Dead Mosquito
at a Time

ALEX PERRY

To Jennifer,
Thanks for the interest!
You bought three!
Alex.

PUBLICAFFAIRS
New York

First published in the United Kingdom in 2011
by C. Hurst & Co. (Publishers) Ltd.

Published in the United States in 2011 by PublicAffairs™,
a Member of the Perseus Books Group

PublicAffairs books are available at special discounts for
bulk purchases in the US by corporations, institutions, and
other organizations. For more information, please contact
the Special Markets Department at the Perseus Books
Group, 2300 Chestnut Street, Suite 200, Philadelphia, PA
19103, call (800) 810-4145, ext. 5000, or e-mail
special.markets@perseusbooks.com.

Book design by Brent Wilcox

Library of Congress Cataloging-in-Publication Data
Perry, Alex.
    Lifeblood : how to change the world, one dead
mosquito at a time / Alex Perry.—1st ed.
        p.   cm.
    Includes bibliographical references and index.
    ISBN 978-1-61039-086-6 (hardback : alk. paper)—
ISBN 978-1-61039-087-3 (e-book)   1. Malaria—
Prevention—Africa.   2. Epidemics—Africa.
3. International cooperation—Africa. I. Title.
RA644.M2P47 2011
614.5'32—dc23
                                        2011024350

First Edition
10 9 8 7 6 5 4 3 2 1

For Tess

They sprayed and sprayed till their eyes got sore

Then they refilled their machines and sprayed some more.

They worked most of the whole night through.

Killing mosquitoes for me and for you.

Their labors resulted in great success.

Of every one hundred mosquitoes, there were ninety-nine less.

But they were mocked and they were scorned,

Their heads with criticism were adorned.

What could be the problem then?

That such reward befell these men?

This answer is simple as numbers can be.

And the calculations reveal for all to see.

That if ninety-nine percent of one billion are slain.

Ten million of the devils still remain.

–Matt Yates
President, American Mosquito Control Association

Contents

Malaria-free countries and malaria-endemic countries in phase of control*, pre-elimination, elimination and prevention of reintroduction, end 2008

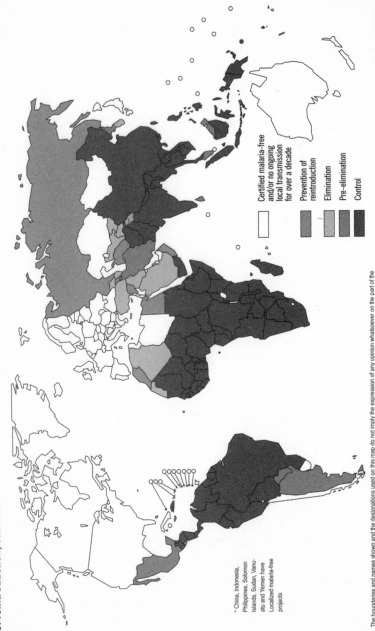

* China, Indonesia, Philippines, Solomon Islands, Sudan, Vanuatu and Yemen have Localized malaria-free projects

Certified malaria-free and/or no ongoing local transmission for over a decade

Prevention of reintroduction

Elimination

Pre-elimination

Control

The boundaries and names shown and the designations used on this map do not imply the expression of any opinion whatsoever on the part of the World Health Organization concerning the legal status of any country, territory, city or area or of its authorities, or concerning the delimitation of its frontiers or boundaries. Dotted lines on maps represent approximate border lines for which there may not yet be full agreement.

This map is intended as a visual aid only and not as a definitive source of information about malaria endemicity.

Data Source: World Malaria Report 2009

World Health Organization

Preface

Does aid work? As a journalist working in the developing world—for three years in the Far East, five years in India, and now four more in Africa—I spend a lot of time trying to answer that question, and many hours sifting press releases from aid groups claiming heroic progress. I first heard about the malaria campaign in the usual way: an April 2009 email from a London PR executive, Rebecca Ladbury, asking whether I would be interested in writing about the launch of a new charity, Malaria No More UK. Ladbury explained the group had been jointly founded by "Wall Street pioneer Ray Chambers, now UN Special Envoy for Malaria" and Peter Chernin, then president of News Corporation. Chambers and Chernin had "decided to apply their private sector expertise and considerable networks to tackle the world's biggest solvable health crisis." After founding Malaria No More in the United States in 2006, they were broadening their scope, launching a British branch at a conference, held at Wilton Park in southern England, on malaria and efforts to fight it. The event was bringing together experts on the disease from all over the world.

The phrase "solvable health crisis" stood out. That meant, presumably, that Chambers and Chernin aimed to end malaria. Sure enough, the email went on to say that the two were part of a campaign that wanted "to end malaria deaths in our lifetime." I called Ladbury.

"Let me make sure I've got this right," I said. "Your clients are trying to kill malaria?"

"Right," said Ladbury.

"That would save millions of lives," I said. "It would be about the single biggest boost to health and development the world has ever seen. It would be astounding."

"Right," repeated Ladbury, a little impatiently. "Do you want me to set up some interviews?"

I did. The ambition was breathtaking. Malaria was one of the world's biggest diseases. It affected half the planet and killed a million people a year. But over the next three days, as Ladbury dragged ever more delegates to the telephone at Wilton Park to speak to me, I realized it wasn't just the campaign's aspiration that set it apart. There were religious leaders at Wilton Park. African health ministers. A smattering of celebrities. Business in particular appeared to be playing a central role: many of the people I was speaking to were senior managers at the world's biggest corporations and talked about running their campaign as though it were a business.

When eventually I spoke to Chambers, he described fighting malaria in terms of efficiency, investment, and returns. His focus was to be "as aggressive as possible to bring deaths as close to zero as possible." This was as much about "economic cost" as "humanitarian cost," he added. "Malaria costs Africa $30–$40 billion each year," he said. "Fixing it is in everyone's interest." The key to that, he added, was a universal, global distribution of bed nets treated with insecticide. "When the mosquito lands on the net, she dies. In areas where we have completed net distributions, deaths go down to zero. We can prevent this disease. This is the greatest opportunity any of us will have in our lifetimes. It's outstanding. And it's doable."

Aid types normally didn't use words like "aggressive" or "opportunity" or even, much, "doable." Malaria was traditionally viewed as a humanitarian concern. Chambers saw it equally as an economic one. My curiosity was piqued. And in the months that followed, I set out to track the campaign. I wanted to plot not only its progress but also its innovations. At first, I was simply pursuing a journalist's hunch that this was a big story. Later, I was able to say why: it opened the door to a new way of aid.

Aid and development are increasingly mired in scandals over inefficiency and corruption, fueling a debate about whether such external assistance does any good at all. The malaria campaign was different in its fresh thinking, particularly the way in which it drew heavily from business. Its results were unusual too: Chambers said malaria was down by two-thirds in Zambia, by 60 percent in Rwanda, by half in Ethiopia, and by close to 100 percent on the Tanzanian island of Zanzibar. And as the months and years passed, during which I watched Chambers go to work in funding forums and aid conferences, and African hospitals and villages, I realized his campaign offered something extraordinary to the aid world: reinvention, even salvation.

There are thousands of people trying to defeat malaria, and it would take a very long book to mention them all. I am also aware that others involved in the work may feel, quite reasonably, that by focusing on Chambers and the group around him, I am denying them their due credit in the pages that follow. So let me be clear: this is not an attempt to document the entirety of the global campaign to kill malaria. Rather, this book tells the story of a small group of people who found themselves at the center of that campaign, whose new ideas and energy were crucial to its remarkable success, and who, I believe, have much to teach us about effective aid. By singling out Chambers and his team, however, I have no wish to downplay the role of others, and any offense is unintentional.

But my initial instinct turned out to be right. Chambers's story is exceptional, with lessons not just for the aid world, but for all of us. Like an infinite army of tiny vampires, mosquitoes were killing close to a million people a year across Africa. And in days lost to fever, and money wasted on medicine that otherwise might have bought a mobile phone or seeds or an education, mosquitoes were taking a giant financial bite out of Africa too, making it dependent on Western charity. Fixing malaria would save lives, but it would save money as well, in Africa and the West. In the beginning, I was planning a story about blood-borne disease and Africans. By the end, I had something much more: a tale about Africa's lifeblood.

CHAPTER 1

Great Lake of Disease

To reach the most malarious place on earth, head north from Kampala, cross the Victoria Nile at Karuma Falls, and just before you come to the refugee camps that mark the southern edge of Uganda's twenty-year civil war, bear right into the vast swamps on the western edge of Lake Kwania. Unlike Africa's other Great Lakes, known for their fresh water beaches and cool evenings, Kwania is a poor place to live. It is wide, stretching sixty miles from its eastern end to the rocky sluice at its western tip, through which it pours into the White Nile. But it is shallow, generally no more than waist-deep, and choked with lilies, papyrus, and water hyacinth, and it has no shoreline: the point where land and water meet is lost in miles of ponds and creeks that resemble ten thousand silver fish bones from the air. Swamps are bad for farming and even worse for fishing. Kwania's miserly depth means even miles out in the open water, the shallow floor can kick up breakers big enough to flip a dugout. And Kwania is full of crocodiles.

Worse danger lurks on land. Kwania's warm, stagnant creeks combine all the conditions guaranteed to sustain an everlasting epidemic of malaria. On the lake's northern edge, the town of Apac turns out to be a particularly good place to culture the malaria parasite: no nearby big cities with public health programs, plus a dense population of warm-blooded creatures on the few pieces of dry land, which form an all but inexhaustible blood bank in which to breed and multiply. Apac also has ideal conditions for propagating malaria's carrier, the mosquito: a consistent equatorial climate of heat and rain, no high mountains to attract snow, and just enough of a breeze off Kwania on which to float a billion bugs. The area is a favorite of one of the deadliest subspecies of mosquito, *Anopheles funestus*. Over millions of years, the *funestus* has evolved into a bloodsucker that feeds almost exclusively on humans. Its appetite is voracious. Researchers in Apac have found each *funestus* fly will bite human flesh around a hundred ninety times a night.[1]

My interest in Apac has been growing since early 2009, when I first began following the new campaign to wipe malaria off the planet. Malaria is our oldest and most widespread disease, almost as old as life itself and far older than humankind. For all our sophistication, more than three billion people still lived with it, every year five hundred million were catching it, and nearly a million were dying from it. It seemed unlikely that a disease so mature and widespread could have retained a center. And yet here in Africa's Rift Valley, where humans first walked out onto the savannah, it had. A trip to Apac seemed like a journey to confront an ancient curse: not Original Sin, certainly, but perhaps Original Sickness. Moreover, if I wanted to know why killing malaria was important and how hard it might be, it seemed a good idea to see how bad it could get. The toxicity was unimaginable. I had tried to imagine living in a place where the average person is bitten tens of thousands of times a year by mosquitoes, of which 1,586—4 bites a day—resulted in infection by malaria,[2] but I couldn't. So in August 2009, I visited Apac.

Research into malaria had already taken me from Cambodia to the Democratic Republic of Congo (DRC), from Zanzibar to Zambia to Zimbabwe. Along the way I had developed a rule of thumb to gauge my chances of being infected. Malaria is a particularly bad risk, it turned out, in places beginning with a K. In Africa, there was Kigali, Kibuye, Kivu, Kinshasa, Kisangani, Kisumu, Kilifi, Kampala, and Karonga on the western shore of Lake Malawi, where in a month's time South African scientists would discover a new type of *funestus*. In Asia, there was Khe Sanh, where US marines found the disease as deadly as the Vietcong in a seventy-seven-day siege during the Tet offensive in 1968; the Burmese hills of the Kayah, Kachin, and Karen, where cerebral malaria is particularly bad; and the Khmer heartland on the Thai-Cambodia border, whose forests have twice turned medicine upside down by producing drug-resistant strains of the parasite. So it was with some foreboding that on studying a map I realized the road to Apac took me from Kampala to Kigumba, onto Karuma via Kitwanga, before turning right on the dirt road to Kwania.

Since I arrive in Apac in the late afternoon, my priority should be finding a netted room. But as I enter the town, I am distracted by a naked man lumbering toward me. He makes no attempt to cover himself and gives no indication he knows he is exposed. He is tall, thin, and filthy. His skin is gray with dust and his ragged hair sprinkled with twigs and dry grass. You might expect a naked man to attract a crowd, but there is no one else around. I approach the man slowly in my car and edge around him. He is talking to someone only he can see. He doesn't appear to register me.

I am still watching him in my rearview mirror when a second naked figure lurches out from a side street. Aside from a torn yellowed cloth slung over his shoulder, the second man looks identical to the first. The same emaciated frame, the same raw and cracked skin at the knees and elbows. Spittle stretches between his dry lips as he mouths his own unintelligible mantra. Ahead, I can make out a third naked figure, sitting in the dust by the side of the road, holding his head in his hands. I keep driving. The third man groans as I pass. I can't shake the thought that I've arrived in a town of zombies.

I decide to stay in the car until I have a better grip on what's going on. In five minutes, I have covered every street in Apac. The town consists of the main road on which I entered, three parallel roads of several hundred yards, and a handful of cross alleys. Aside from the three naked men, I haven't seen a soul. Eventually I find myself outside a building whose sign announces it is the district headquarters of the health ministry. I pull into the empty car lot, walk in through the entrance, and find my way down a dark corridor to a door marked "District Health Officer." I knock. A voice asks me to enter.

Behind two sets of fly screens and under a ceiling fan, Dr. Matthew Emer is at his desk. I introduce myself and explain my interest in malaria. Dr. Emer offers me a seat and a glass of water, and asks how he can help.

Who are the naked men wandering around outside? *What* are they?

"Brain damage," Dr. Emer replies. "Severe malaria can do that to a baby. You never recover."[3]

Dr. Emer thinks I should see some statistics. The district of Apac has a population of 515,500. Between July 2008 and June 2009, 124,538 people sought treatment for malaria. I note the figure of 124,538 includes 58,632 children below the age of five. Malaria targets the very young, whose immunity has not had a chance to build, and the pregnant, whose immunity drops away so that the fetus is not flooded with adult-strength antibodies.

Dr. Emer pulls out a bar chart showing that his staff deals with around 3,000 cases of malaria a week, rising to 5,000 in the worst weeks. The 2008–2009 numbers, I note, are actually an improvement on the previous year. Then 148,082 people were diagnosed with malaria, of whom 67,281 were children under five. That means that in 2007–2008, 7 out of every 10 small children in Apac contracted malaria.

Over the next three days, I learn how Dr. Emer's staff is underfunded, underpaid, undersupplied with out-of-date drugs, and undertrained on how to use them. For now, Dr. Emer feels it enough to mention the chronic understaffing. He has just three of the seven doctors he needs for his hospital, and he is missing a third of the nurses and assistants he requires for his thirty-seven clinics.

What does so much disease do to a place? Dr. Emer explains that contracting malaria is often just the beginning of someone's troubles. Malaria might kill you. But if it doesn't, it is generally the start of a long cycle of illness and poverty. "Because kids get malaria, there is a lot of absence from school," he says. "So our kids don't do well. So they don't get good jobs, and they don't earn money. Then they have children, who also get sick, and the parents have to spend their little money on them instead of spending it on schools or other things—and they also have to stay home to look after them, so they lose more money. Malaria keeps us poor." And if malaria breeds poverty, poverty boosts malaria. "Say every house has five children, and each child has five to ten episodes of malaria a year," says Dr. Emer. "And Coartem [the malaria cure] costs $8 to $10. That's up to $500 a year for someone who earns $1 a day or less."

Dr. Emer watches me jot down the figures in my notepad.

"That doesn't add up," I say, finally.

"It doesn't add up," repeats Dr. Emer.

"What happens to the children whose parents can't afford Coartem?" I ask.

"They die," replies Dr. Emer.

"Do people accept this?" I ask. "That malaria will inevitably kill some of their children?"

For a moment, I think Dr. Emer is going to hit me. Then he says, tightly: "People do not accept it. Something kills your child, this is not something that can be accepted. They are always asking for bed nets. They are always asking us, 'When are you going to spray?' When Kampala sends us Coartem, we finish it in one day."

I thank Dr. Emer and ask him to recommend a hotel in town with nets in the windows. "Just give *us* nets," he says as I leave. "Just give us the medicines so we can manage this."

I drive to the Lamco B Self-Contained Rooms, a dirty, single-story tin-roofed building that is located, as Dr. Emer said, just past the One Step Bar. The streets are still empty. Only the insane or the newly arrived, I surmise, spend much time out of doors in Apac. Not that there is much to go out for. Among the items on the One Step's menu is "Dry Pest Meat with Cassava" for $1.50. Neither that nor the two prostitutes slumped across its tiny bar have attracted a single customer.

Inside the Lamco I am shown behind reception to an internal, windowless courtyard and a door that opens onto a small, equally windowless sitting room, a smaller bedroom, and a tiny attached shower, mine for $3 a night. The bed has a newish-looking net over it, but the screen across the bedroom window, which looks onto a back alley, is torn, and the window won't close. I find a hole in the shower wall through which I can see clear into the alley. It is filled with rubbish. The toilet is stained and smells stagnant. I try the shower and receive a sharp electric shock from the metal tap. Using a T-shirt wrapped around my hand to work the tap, I wash, cover myself with mosquito repellent, put on a pair of long socks, jeans, and a long-sleeved sweatshirt, take my Malarone pill, get under the net, and lie sweating in the nearly 90-degree heat until I fall asleep.

The next morning, with a handful of fresh bites on my neck, I drive to Apac District Hospital. The district hospital represents the highest of the four levels of medical care in the Ugandan public health system. On the building's steps I find Alele Quinto, a young clinical officer, who offers to show me around. He takes me to the pediatric ward and, in a side office, shows me the admissions book. I read the entries.

OMARA RONALD
  Age: 1 and a quarter. Male. 9 kg. Malaria. i/v 5% Dextrose, Quinine 10mg, Quinine Syrup 5 mls, 250mg Panadol.
OWINY LABAKA ABDIRICHAN
  4 months. Male. 5kg. Malaria. i/v 5% Dextrose, Quinine 10mg, Quinine Syrup 5 mls, 250mg Panadol.
AKAKI AGAI ABDANI
  6 months. Male. 8kg. Malaria. i/v 5% Dextrose, Quinine 10mg, Quinine Syrup 5 mls, 250mg Panadol.

ADANG LOG ROMA
4 months. Female. 2.4kg. i/v 5% Dextrose, Quinine 10mg,
Quinine Syrup 5 mls, 250mg Panadol.

All babies, all with malaria, all admitted that morning. The previous day there were seven; the day before, nineteen. The treatment is just as alarming. Quinine was phased out in the rich world long ago, after the malaria parasite became resistant. In the most malarious town on earth, the staff at its district hospital are fighting the disease with old medicine, sugar solution, and headache pills.

Alele takes me to the children's ward. On entering, we are hit by a warm, sweet stench. There are forty beds in two cramped lines on either side of the room. On each bed are a mother and baby. Relatives squat and lie on the floor. There are no nets over the beds, no fans, and no screens on the ward's windows, which are wide open. Through one window, I see a child wander outside, squat, and defecate yellow diarrhea onto the ground. Behind him, mothers pound cassava and hang up clothes to dry. Goats and chickens wander through. I notice a tiny tornado of mosquitoes hanging over every bed on the ward. If a child doesn't have malaria when he or she arrives, the child seems sure to contract the disease during his or her stay.

Alele introduces me to Judith Adongo, who is on one of the beds cuddling a small baby. Judith is twenty-three and lives with her husband, James, on their small maize and cassava plantation in the swamps. She tells me her four-year-old son, Oscar, has contracted severe malaria seven times. Now it is the turn of his nine-month-old sister, Monica, who is vomiting and running a high fever. I ask James, twenty-seven, how many children he wants. "I need at least five," he laughs. Then, suddenly serious: "But since malaria is always there, I may have to look for one or two more." In my reporting, I have become used to hearing the cynical view that malaria is nature's solution to overpopulation. James's calculations suggest just the opposite.

Back in admissions, I meet Sister Adebo Rose. She is trying to find a vein on the back of a baby girl's hand in which to insert an intravenous drip. Malaria can kill in hours. Mostly, says Sister Adebo, a sick child's parents, particularly those who can ill afford treatment, will wait until the last moment before making the trip to the hospital, by which time the child's veins have collapsed from dehydration. Locating a deflated, child-size vein is hard, and eventually Sister Adebo gives up stabbing the girl's tiny hands and tries the side of her head. The child, terrified, screams throughout. I ask Sister Adebo if the work ever gets to her. She looks at me blankly. "We see them die," she replies finally. "A lot die."

Alele takes me to the maternity ward. It is the same—overcrowded, and all but one of the patients suffering from malaria. I am prepared for suffering, but the sight of a ward of expectant mothers, none rosy-cheeked, none excited, all sick, all way too thin, is still shocking. To try to bring new life into a place like Apac, I realize, is to open the gates to death.

After showing me around, Alele wants to talk. He has finished secondary school and has ambitions to become a doctor. He has read in a Ugandan newspaper that Apac has the highest rates of malaria transmission in the world. "Some countries are in the news because of their new wealth," he says. "But in Apac, it's because of disease." I tell him my own country, Britain, wiped out malaria half a century before. "No malaria?" he exclaims. "Fifty years ago! Ah! Imagine!" He suddenly looks worried. "We are scared of people who come here from the outside, from places without malaria," he says. "Every visitor, they get sick. One mosquito bite is enough to put you down forever."

A never-ending malaria epidemic is enough to put an entire town down forever. Whereas other human settlements are shaped by their proximity to a navigable river or a natural harbor, or perhaps the discovery of oil or diamonds or gold, Apac is fashioned by malaria. The disease has put a stranglehold on almost any development. What economy does exist is based around administering to the sick and the dead. A five-minute walk down Apac's main street—Hospital Road—takes me past twelve medical centers, ten pharmacists, and the Nightingale Comprehensive School of Nursing, housed in a crumbling, windowless, single-story brick building. In between is an array of churches and mosques, many with a homemade feel, such as the tiny wood shack on a street behind the Lamco whose sign reveals it is the Voice of Salvation and Healing Church. Even the names of the few general businesses in town—the Sunset Lodge and the Die Hard Electrical Store—seem to have double meanings.

Apac, very obviously, has a problem. Yet somehow the world has missed it. Signs erected by the side of the road announce the presence of two foreign assistance programs. In a place where malaria can kill hundreds of children a day, the office for a child protection program funded by Germany and the European Union has no malaria program but concentrates instead on what it calls "gender-based violence." Signs for the Republic of Uganda's National Wetlands Program, funded by the Belgian Technical Cooperation in Uganda, urge residents to "Protect Wetland. It is our water granary. It stores, filters and purifies." In case anyone wonders where the program stands on the question of wetness versus human life, it has erected other signs next to stagnant ditches around town that read: "Water Drainage Prohibited." By banning people from draining the swamps in which their future death is spawned, the program says it is "empowering development."

Later Dr. Emer tells me about another benign-sounding foreign initiative: organic farming. In early 2008, he says, he sprayed 103,025 houses in Apac with insecticide, a program paid for by the World Health Organization and other foreign donors. His figures show malaria almost immediately halved. Yet after three months, a court told him to stop. Why? Objections from Uganda's organic cotton farmers, who supply Nike, H&M, and Wal-Mart's George Baby line. The farmers claimed their foreign buyers could not have chemicals anywhere near their cotton if it was to be certified as organic. Chemical-free farming in Africa probably sounds like a great idea in the West, remarks Dr. Emer. The reality is that African babies are dying so that Western babies can wear organic.

Back at the Lamco, I strike up a conversation with the owner, Lameck Abongo. "Business is terrible," says Lameck, who is sixty-two. "People don't come to town. Visitors from the villages just come for small things and go back by night. From Kampala they also just come for the day and make sure they're gone by dark. And nobody comes at all unless they have a very good reason. Why would they? This is a place of suffering. When you are here, you do not enjoy. In life you need to enjoy, but it's not possible here."[4]

What persuaded him to open a hotel in the most malaria-infected place on earth?

Lameck shifts uncomfortably. He *had* got out when he was younger, he says. For a decade, he ran a dry goods store in Lira, a city two hours away. The business did well. He sent all his eight surviving children (two daughters died of malaria) to schools in

Kampala. Then he moved back to Apac and opened up the Lamco. He had high hopes for a family business: Lamco is an acronym for the "Lameck Abongo and Martin Company," Martin being Lameck's eldest son. Before the Lamco B, there had been Lamco A, another guesthouse; lack of demand later forced him to turn it into a dispensary. "It was after they built the hospital here," says Lameck of his move to Apac. "State money seemed to be coming in, and I was convinced by a top official that Apac would be the best. 'If you go to Apac, you will be rich,' he said. 'The government is investing there.'"

It didn't happen. The official soon disappeared to Kampala. "I think he died," says Lameck. "I think maybe he died of malaria."

I return twice more to the hospital. The rains have started, and I want to see their effect. By the time I return that night, another ten babies have been admitted. The sweet-sickly smell has intensified, and the ward is spilling over with children and parents. In a corridor, three mothers cradle their babies as Martin, a twenty-seven-year-old orderly, brings them one by one into the small admissions room and tries to fit them with drips. Martin is the only member of staff on duty. He isn't coping. I watch him try to stick a needle into a four-month-old girl, Doris Amang. He uses a tourniquet to try to raise a vein on the back of one of Doris's hands, then the other. Next he tries both sides of Doris's head. She screams and kicks. Martin tries to hold his hand over her eyes and turn her head away. Twice he sends her back into the corridor to calm down. Eventually, after pricking her ten or twelve times, he gives up. The windows are wide open. As I watch, a mosquito buzzes around his head and settles on Doris's cheek.

After a second night at the Lamco, and sporting more bites, I wish Lameck good luck, check out of my room, and head to the hospital for a final visit. Martin is long gone. There are no other staff. A rough head count confirms ten more kids have arrived, making fifty in all. The ward is out of beds, and the new arrivals are sleeping on flattened cardboard boxes in the corridor.

I realize the mothers are looking to me. I have nothing to offer them. I leave the ward, walk quickly to my car, and drive for the gates. Ahead of me is a naked street walker, feeling his way along the fence. As I roar past him, I catch a glimpse of a startled, emaciated expression. I turn onto Hospital Road and drive back through town. I race through the empty streets. I don't stop until I reach Kampala.

CHAPTER 2

Original Sickness

Malaria covers the globe. It stunts whole continents. As well as killing one million people a year, it infects two hundred fifty million to five hundred million more. In lost work days, unnecessary expense, and wasted potential, the development economist Jeffrey Sachs reckons it costs Africa $12 billion a year, a figure Ray Chambers has revised to $30 to $40 billion. Fixing malaria would, no doubt, be a colossal boost to health and development. But that begs the question: why hasn't it been done? The answer is stark: malaria is the oldest challenge in medicine because it is one of the hardest. Many scientists and development specialists doubt it can be done.

Compared to malaria, humans are evolution's gate-crasher. Scientists date the origins of the disease to microscopic protozoa that existed hundreds of millions of years ago, long before the birth of most species. Those protozoa would most likely have lived in water as plantlike algae—hence some cells in the modern malaria parasite still carry plastids, genomes that indicate a previous ability to photosynthesize. Living alongside insect eggs and larvae on the water's surface, these ancestors of malaria gradually adapted to become parasites living in the guts of those larvae.

Further evolution followed. When larvae became insects and took flight, malaria went with them. When warm-blooded animals arrived, and when female mosquitoes became bloodsuckers, the malaria parasite adapted to live inside red blood cells—where it was protected from its new host's immune system. And when insects began to specialize in different blood sources—birds, lizards, mice, rabbits, bats, squirrels, porcupines, monkeys, apes, and people—so did the malaria parasite. Today, after eons of evolution, there are four hundred fifty different recognized species of the malaria parasite *Plasmodium*, and another is identified every few years.

The human malaria parasite is especially complex. It is composed of around five thousand genes and during the course of its life takes on seven distinct forms on its journey from mosquito gut to human bloodstream and back again. Those changes account for the delay in the appearance of the disease's symptoms— a person bitten by a malarious mosquito will not come down with fever until after the parasite has traversed the bloodstream, infected the liver, multiplied, then burst back out into the bloodstream, a process that takes a minimum of six days. These shape-shifting properties are also one reason why the disease has proved so hard to beat.[1]

Several thousand years ago, two dominant strains of human malaria parasite emerged, *Plasmodium falciparum* and *Plasmodium vivax*, with the former the more deadly and widespread of the two.[2] At the time, organized agriculture was spreading from the Fertile Crescent in the Middle East to Africa. Humans were leaving behind a hunter-gatherer existence and settling into densely populated villages, often in cleared tropical forest and next to water. That was a stroke of luck for the local Anopheles mosquito: not only had humans stopped moving and now presented themselves as stationary targets, but they were doing so close to the rivers and lakes in which mosquitoes could breed. The Anopheles population exploded. So, naturally, did malaria.

From Africa, *Plasmodium falciparum* and *vivax* spread out across the world. Epidemiologists measure a disease's contagiousness by a reproductive number—the number of cases one would expect to see from a single founding case. Malaria turns out to be the world's most contagious disease, with a reproductive number of anywhere from 10 to 3,000. (By comparison, the reproductive number for H1N1, or swine flu, is 3.)[3]

The key to malaria's wide spread is not the virus itself nor its carrier, the mosquito, which can only fly five miles and live for two weeks. It is us. Humans travel further and wider than any other animal. And as Africans ventured out into the world, wherever they went, they carried the malaria parasite in their blood. China might have known about malaria 5,000 years ago: the 4,700-year-old canon of Chinese medicine, the *Nei Ching*, mentions recurring fevers that enlarge spleens, classic symptoms of malaria. Texts dating from the same time found in Sumeria (now Iraq) and Egypt also speak of malarialike fevers. Evidence of *falciparum* was found too in 40 percent of the collection of Egyptian mummies at the Turin Museum, which date from 3200 BC.[4] Over the millennia, the disease spread around the Mediterranean and into Europe, reaching northern Europe in the Dark Ages. It moved onto the Americas a few centuries later with the advent of colonization and the accompanying trade in African slaves.

Malaria's global reach has given it an unprecedented impact on human history.[5] Moving east to west, in Asia malaria is thought to have stopped Alexander the Great in India in 326 BC and killed Genghis Khan a millennium and a half later. In Asia and Africa, it determined patterns of colonization and development. Malaria made the tropical forests, thick bush, and swamps of much of Africa's interior a no-go area for Europeans—60 percent of missionaries sent to West Africa between 1804 and 1825 perished[6]—and to this day, big cities on the continent either cling to the coast or, in the interior, to high ground. But while malaria killed off European explorers, it allowed the comparatively malaria-immune Bantu tribes from West Africa to spread east and south. Their descendants—the Kikuyu in Kenya, the Shona in Zimbabwe, and the Xhosa and Zulu in South Africa—remain dominant today.

Further north in Egypt, malaria killed the boy pharaoh Tutankhamen in 1324 BC.[7] In Italy, it determined who ruled much of the known world. Malaria precipitated the first fall of Rome, so weakening its defenders that they were unable to beat back attacks by the barbarian Prince Alaric in 410 AD—then decimated Alaric's forces as well. It prompted the relocation of the Vatican in 1574 after the death of numerous popes and, centuries later, helped spur mass Italian emigration to the United States. So associated was malaria with Italy that the disease took an Italian name: "mal'aria," meaning bad air, after the foul swamp vapors originally thought to carry it.

Across the English Channel in Britain, malaria killed Oliver Cromwell in 1658 and nearly claimed his royal successor Charles II during a London malaria epidemic in 1678. A few decades later, it helped end Scottish independence: so devastated by the disease were late-seventeenth-century Scottish settlers hoping to colonize the lush, fertile jungles of Panama that it ruined the finances of their homeland and, in 1707, forced Scotland to accept English rule in return for London's assumption of its debts. Once inside the Americas, malaria went on to infect eight presidents, the last of which was John F. Kennedy. It also helped set the tone for centuries of racial antagonism. In the eighteenth and nineteenth centuries, African slaves' superior immunity to the disease propelled their population to majorities in the southern states. The threat such a numerical advantage implied sowed the seeds of segregation, a system originally conceived by the white ruling elite as a defensive response to the end of slavery. Some say malaria even explains how the nation of the 1773 Boston Tea Party became today's land of the latte: in the nineteenth century, coffee, which has a chemical structure and bitter taste similar to quinine, was widely believed to protect against the disease.[8]

Malaria, then, is perpetual, a global scourge, a driver of human history, even a determinant of human evolution. To this day, a third of West Africans have sickle cell anemia, an often deadly mutation of red blood cells that might have been eliminated through natural selection but for the protection it offers against the most severe attacks of malaria.[9]

If much human history can be told through the story of malaria, that's just as true with the annals of medicine. The Western world's first physician, Hippocrates, lived from 460 to 370 BC in ancient Greece and earned that title from his studies of malaria. He was the first to distinguish malaria from other types of fever, such as typhoid. Some of his conclusions were wide of the mark: he claimed there were two types of malaria fever, those that fell on even days and those falling on odd days. More accurately, he noted the disease's ability to enlarge the spleen and made a connection between it, the marshes outside Athens, and the onset of rain in the autumn.[10]

It would be another two thousand years before the disease was associated not with stagnant water and its vapors but with the mosquitoes that bred in it. But then, in the late nineteenth century, the discoveries came all at once. In 1880 Frenchman Charles Louis Alphonse Laveran identified the malaria parasite in a military hospital in Algeria—though he was initially widely disbelieved. In 1885, Italian Camillo Golgi established there was more than one type of malaria. And in a series of experiments in 1897 and 1898, a British imperial physician, Surgeon Major Ronald Ross, discovered the malaria parasite in the dissected gut of a mosquito that had bitten a malarious patient, thus proving how malaria is transmitted. Also in 1898, an Italian biologist, Giovanni Battista Grassi, did the same by passing malaria into a human volunteer through the bite of an infected mosquito. Ross was awarded the Nobel Prize for medicine in 1902. Laveran won the same prize for his work on malaria in 1907.

Despite not knowing how malaria worked until the late nineteenth century, by then we had already been treating it successfully for hundreds of years. In 1631, a Jesuit apothecary in Peru called Agostino Salumbrino sent back to Rome the bitter bark from the cinchona tree, explaining that Peruvians used it as a cure for fever. As Fiammetta Rocco writes in her history of cinchona, *The Miraculous Fever Tree*, its alkaloid extract, quinine, became "the modern world's first real pharmaceutical drug."[11] A later synthetic version, chloroquine, became the ubiquitous malaria treatment of the twentieth century. In time, the antimalarial properties of an extract of the Chinese sweet wormwood tree, artemisinin, would also become known to a wider world.

After Laveran, Grassi, and Ross had shown how malaria was transmitted, we could not only treat malaria but also prevent it. As more was discovered about mosquitoes, we learned males were harmless, feeding on nectar and plant juices, and only females needed the nutrients of a blood meal to produce eggs. Female Anopheles had adapted themselves to feeding almost exclusively on humans, generally at night when their prey was asleep and stationary. They located their victims with sensors that followed heat and the plume of carbon dioxide in a person's breath. In theory, that made prevention easy. For people: a nighttime regimen of long-sleeved shirts, full-length pants, and socks and hanging nets around beds. For the landscape: the draining of marshes, swamps, and ponds; the oiling of puddles; the fumigating of buildings and hedgerows; and the screening of doors and windows.

Straightforward, perhaps. But given malaria's global spread and the limited resources of the time, unfeasible. As Richard Feachem, the first executive director of the Global Fund to Fight AIDS, Tuberculosis and Malaria, says: "People forget today, but even as recently as the end of World War II, every country in the world had endemic malaria transmission within its borders, even inside the Arctic Circle."[12] Eradication efforts initially concentrated on limited areas where it made economic sense. The first took place in Panama, scene of Scotland's earlier misfortune. In 1904, the US took on the long-standing project to build a canal between the Atlantic and the Pacific and—since malaria had defeated all previous attempts—employed a US military doctor, William Crawford Gorgas, to purify the area. The campaign was abhorrent in its selectivity. Gorgas included white managers and overseers in his efforts but excluded black laborers, who subsequently died in the thousands.

But Gorgas's efforts succeeded as far as they went: malaria and yellow fever deaths among whites plummeted, the Panama Canal was completed in 1914, and the narrow exclusion zones in which whites lived and worked remained malaria-free for decades.[13]

In Europe and the US in the early twentieth century, malaria also declined rapidly. This was due not just to health campaigns. Mosquitoes' opportunities to breed were also being reduced by the draining of swampland for pasture and the mechanization of agriculture, which prompted former farm workers to migrate en masse to the cities.[14] But the malarious battlefields of World War II—around the Mediterranean and in the Middle East and Southeast Asia—forced the disease back onto the health agenda once more. In 1944, malaria even held up the Allied advance north through Italy after the German army purposefully caused an outbreak by flooding the land around Rome and confiscating local stockpiles of antimalarial drugs. In response to the threat, the US Army recruited Theodor Seuss Geisel, better known as Dr. Seuss, to produce a cartoon pamphlet for the troops featuring a sultry Anopheles drinking what appeared to be a glass of red wine. "This is Ann," wrote Seuss.

> She drinks blood! Her full name is Anopheles Mosquito and she's dying to meet you! Ann moves around at night (a real party gal) and she's got a thirst. No whiskey, gin, beer or rum coke for Ann. She drinks G.I. blood. She can make you feel like a combination of a forest fire, a January blizzard, and an old dish mop . . . and now and then she can knock you flat for keeps. . . . If you go running around like a strip-teaser, you haven't got a chance. Bathing and swimming at night where Ann hangs out really is asking for trouble. Head nets,

rolled-down sleeves, leggings and gloves may seem like sissy stuff and not so comfortable—BUT a guy out cold from MALARIA is just as stiff as the one who stopped a hunk of steel. . . . Now IF you really are looking for trouble and you don't want to miss [out]—just drop down to the nearest native village some evening. The places are lousy with fat little Anns sitting around waiting for you with their bellies full of germs. They stock up on MALARIA bugs from the hometown boys and gals and when they find a nice new sucker they give him the works. So, lay off the native villages if you want to keep the top of your head on. . . . She'll bat you down and it won't be funny.[15]

The US Army wanted GIs to cover up. But its generals also knew the best way to fight a war was not protecting your own side but killing the enemy. Carbon, hydrogen, and chlorine had been first synthesized into dichloro-diphenyl-trichloroethane (DDT) in 1874, but it wasn't until 1939 that the Swiss chemist Paul Hermann Müller discovered the chemical's properties as an insecticide. (Müller would also win the 1948 Nobel Prize for medicine for his breakthrough.) In his experiments, Müller showed DDT was a long-lasting poison, lethal to cold-blooded insects, and cheap to produce but, miraculously, seemingly harmless to people. The US Army began using it in 1944. Malaria was quickly beaten back, and Germany and Japan defeated soon afterward.

When the war ended, DDT went on sale to civilians. As GIs returned with tales of the wonder powder, sales rocketed. Backed by government scientists and wild public excitement, farmers set out to exterminate all insects—less because of the risk of malaria, which was now in abeyance, than out of a simple dislike of creepy crawlies.[16] The chemical was sprayed on walls, fields, and swamps and dropped from the air. By 1952 malaria had been eradicated in the US.

Outside the US, the advent of DDT coincided with the birth of foreign aid. In addition to the Marshall Plan, in 1943 the Allies also set up the United Nations Relief and Rehabilitation Administration (UNRRA), the first ever UN organization to administer relief in war zones. That included public health, and in that endeavor they were joined by private philanthropic groups such as the Rockefeller Foundation. After the war, these bodies used DDT to launch a new war on insect-borne disease. In 1946, the expanding UNRRA was split into several more specialized UN agencies, among them the World Health Organization (WHO) and the United Nations Children's Fund (UNICEF). And it was the WHO that initiated the first Global Malaria Eradication Program, in 1955.

Persuaded that US-funded malaria eradication was a way to convince the world that Washington was a more beneficent patron than the Soviet Union, in 1958 the US Congress allocated $100 million for a five-year malaria eradication program, an amount it would increase to a total of $490 million by 1963.[17] The scale of this effort can be measured by the fact that in the early 1960s a total of ninety-three countries, almost half the world, had American-funded malaria eradication programs that used DDT spraying—conducted by hand, from fumigating trucks, and from the air.

The results were spectacular. Cases of malaria fell from 3 million in Sri Lanka in 1946 to 7,300 in 1951 to just 18 in 1963;[18] life expectancy there rose from forty-three years to fifty-seven. In India, infections plummeted from 75 million and 800,000 deaths in 1947 to 100,000 and fewer than 100 deaths in 1965.[19] In Sardinia, an early test, they plunged from a pre-eradication 75,000 cases in the 1940s to 9 in 1951.[20] Over the duration of the campaign, eighteen countries around the world became malaria-free, accounting for 32 percent of humankind. Malaria cases fell from 350 million to 100 million.[21] Our most historic disease, it was confidently predicted, would soon itself be history.

So what happened? Why, half a century after we looked set to rid the planet of malaria, does it still sicken half a billion people a year and kill a million? The uncomfortable truth is that what should have been one of our great successes became one of our greatest failures. After its initial stunning success, the WHO's global eradication campaign ran out of steam. Then it was abandoned altogether.

Why? First, spraying wasn't always popular with the people it was supposed to protect. DDT killed insects, certainly. But it also killed chickens and cats that ate the poisoned bugs. (In an incident lampooned for years afterward by environmentalists, in early 1960 Britain's Royal Air Force parachuted twenty cats in wicker baskets into a remote Borneo village to compensate for those killed by DDT).[22] Teams of sprayers, sent by central governments and foreigners, found a cold welcome. Dispirited, they began overspraying in the mornings so they could stop early or taking bribes not to spray, even selling their DDT in markets. Surveillance teams checking up on the sprayers were similarly uncommitted: many failed to visit remote areas or lacked the skills to collect and analyze blood samples properly. Partly because DDT was not being applied with sufficient thoroughness, partly because DDT was also being used by farmers as a plant pesticide, evolution began to select for survival mosquitoes that were resistant to low levels of DDT. "What didn't kill them only made them stronger," writes the malaria historian Sonia Shah in *The Fever*.[23]

There were other reasons to turn against DDT. Research revealed rising concentrations of the stuff in the food chain. It was killing birds and infecting milk. In 1962, the environmentalist Rachel Carson published *Silent Spring*, which suggested pesticides such as DDT were endangering the entire ecosystem and pushing species such as the bald eagle, the US national bird, to extinction. The book became one of the most influential of the twentieth century. Not only did it change opinion on DDT forever—the US stopped funding the WHO campaign in 1963 and banned the substance altogether in 1972—Carson's vision of the planet as an interconnected, living organism became the intellectual foundation of the ecological movement.

But what doomed the WHO's campaign from the start was that, in reality, it was not global at all. Incredible as it might seem today, the WHO simply left out Africa. The WHO had a procedural excuse for the omission: most of Africa was still under colonial rule, at least at the start of the campaign, and the WHO's mandate did not cover colonies. But there was little mystery as to the real reason. Staff at the WHO wanted a success. So they chose not to include the continent with the worst infrastructure and capacity and that, not coincidentally, had the worst malaria. That heartless, circular logic—we can't help the poorest because their poverty makes it too hard—was matched by the ruthless calculus of the eradication program's main funder. The US deemed Africa less critical to the outcome of the Cold War than, say, Central America or Southeast Asia.[24]

The legacy of the WHO campaign was mixed. By its end, large parts of the world, notably the US, Europe, Russia, and parts of Asia like the Korean peninsula, were malaria-free. Today that list has grown. As Feachem says, the entire planet had malaria in 1945 but now "100 countries have got rid of it, and there are 100 malarious countries."[25]

But in those countries where the disease survived, the campaign bequeathed a more powerful mosquito, inured to DDT, and a malaria parasite increasingly resistant to chloroquine. Unsurprisingly, it rebounded. Sri Lanka was back to 500,000 cases by 1969; India resurged to a million.[26] Worse, in its epicenter of Africa, malaria was untouched. In 1969, the WHO formally dumped eradication as a goal and switched to learning to live with the disease through treatment and scattershot prevention.

The campaign may have failed to kill malaria. But it was murder on malariology. When DDT seemed, at least for a few years, finally to have solved a problem that had dogged medicine for millennia, the field lost much of its interest for doctors. Malariologists changed disciplines. Few new doctors felt the specialty worth pursuing. Within a few years, there was just a handful of practicing malaria experts in the world.

Brian Greenwood shouldn't have been one of them. As a 1962 graduate of London's Middlesex Hospital, Greenwood says he had intended to follow his contemporaries to Harley Street, the exclusive London address of Britain's best private doctors. Greenwood—tall, charming, unfailingly polite—is from that generation of Englishmen who view introspection as poor manners. "Something was not quite right, so in 1965 I went to Africa," is all he will say of the decision that changed his life and those of millions of others. The non sequitur is as apparent to him as anyone. "I still don't know why I did that," he adds.[27]

After a short spell in Zambia, "where I was inspired by independence and [anticolonial leader Kenneth] Kaunda," Greenwood took a job as a medical registrar at a teaching hospital in Ibadan in the sweltering forests of southern Nigeria. Overstaffing in Ibadan—there were eight doctors for thirty patients—left plenty of time for immunology research, which was developing into a passion for Greenwood. He also saw a bright future in African medicine. He expected, he says, "that Africa would soon have a lot more hospitals like that. The indicators at the time showed we were better than Thailand or Singapore."

It wouldn't work out that way. As so often in postindependence Africa, civil war blighted expectations. In 1967 Nigeria was split by the Biafran conflict, which was to last for three years. "The doctors who were Biafrans left, and I suddenly had more responsibility," says Greenwood. Safety was a concern, of course. But the lure of more patients on whom to conduct research was overpowering. Greenwood's studies consumed him. "I began to wonder why autoimmune diseases were so high," he says. "Since malaria had such an impact on the immune system, could the answer be malaria?"

After two years, Greenwood returned to London with the data and samples he had gathered. Three years of lab work proved preventing malaria was key to improving health in Africa: stopping malaria, and so blocking its damaging impact on the immune system, also checked a host of other diseases. "That was it," says Greenwood. "I was hooked by Africa and by malaria. It's such a beautiful and clever parasite. I was offered a master's position in Canada. But they had a new medical school in northern Nigeria, and I went there."

By now Greenwood was not so much choosing a path less trodden as forging one never trodden before. Newly married, with children, he brought his family with him to Africa and the new medical school at Ahmadu Bello University in the remote town of Zaria in the heat and dust on the southern edge of the Sahara. Few other doctors were willing to do the same. In addition to the dubious attractions of specializing in a small and shrinking field and working at a teaching hospital in northern Nigeria, Greenwood couldn't offer much pay. "We struggled," he says. "There was never much money, and we were always fighting off attempts to close us down."

But the obscurity and difficulty of the work acted like a filter for quality. Only the best and most dedicated applied. A small group of malariologists began to gather around Greenwood in Nigeria, and when in 1980 he moved to the Medical Research Council Laboratories in Banjul, Gambia, they followed. Among Greenwood's disciples: Eldryd Parry, future Cambridge professor and founder of the Tropical Health and Education Trust; David Warrell, later president of the Royal Society of Tropical Medicine and Hygiene and professor emeritus at Oxford University; Bob Snow, future professor of tropical public health at Oxford and head of the Malaria Public Health and Epidemiology Group in Nairobi; Kevin Marsh, who now runs the KEMRI-Wellcome Research Programme in Kilifi, Kenya; and Pedro Alonso, who founded the Manhiça Health Research Centre in Mozambique to develop malaria vaccines. "It was definitely not the thing to do," says Greenwood of his small band of malariologists. "You had to be pretty sure that's what you wanted. Most of their colleagues thought these guys were crazy, just stepping off the ladder for a job in a tiny field where you were lucky if you got £20,000 a year. But if you were interested in malaria, there was nowhere else to go, and as a result, we gathered a very small, very dedicated group of experts. Pretty much everybody went on to become famous." Greenwood pauses for a moment of reflection. "I have to say I really enjoyed it. I had a lovely time."

With so few malariologists left in the world, these were golden years for malaria too. Though malaria deaths would never again return to their previous heights of an annual two million at the start of the twentieth century, the burden of the disease was rising steadily. Partly that was because inside malariology, eradication was now viewed as a foolish dream. "We were dominated by the failure of the old campaign," says Marcel Tanner, director of the Swiss Tropical Institute in Basel. "It became obscene to use such words. People said: 'You're stupid; it won't work.'"[28]

Greenwood and his group could still try to alleviate suffering, however. They conducted trials of new artemisinin-based treatments. They also went back to basics, reviving a malaria prevention method that required little skill to distribute or administer: the bed net. "The thing about malaria," says Bob Snow, "is that we know what to do about it, and it's not that sophisticated. We know that you make your children sleep under a bed net. This is not anti-retrovirals for the rest of your life, like HIV. This is easy."[29]

This was also, as the team discovered, surprisingly effective. In the 1980s and 1990s, the Gambian group conducted a series of tests on bed nets they treated with a new insecticide—not the by-now-notorious DDT but permethrin, which also killed mosquitoes on contact. In September 1991, they published their findings: insecticide-treated nets cut malaria deaths among children by 70 percent and overall child deaths by 63 percent.[30] "It was a stunning result," says Christian Lengeler, head of the Health Intervention Unit at the Swiss Tropical Institute. "But they knew that in order to convince people, they had to repeat the trials on a huge scale in other settings."[31]

Over the next five years, Lengeler coordinated four mass trials of bed nets involving tens of thousands of people in Gambia,

Ghana, Burkina Faso, and Kenya. The results were not as impressive as Greenwood's initial data. But their meaning was clear, and profound. "They showed you could bring down child deaths by a fifth," says Lengeler. "After the measles vaccine, there is nothing else in public health that's ever had that kind of impact. And since those trials, we've seen that the true impact is actually much higher, maybe as much as 40 percent."

What really fascinated the malariologists was how deaths kept on falling the more nets were used. The greater the number of nets, the greater the number of dead mosquitoes, the better the transmission of malaria was interrupted. "It's like a downward spiral," says Lengeler. So impressive were the results of blanket net coverage that they suggested a new possibility: covering every bed in one area might kill so many mosquitoes that malaria itself would be eliminated forever. It stood to reason. If all the mosquitoes were dead, and the area was so big that other mosquitoes could not penetrate it, then malaria was dead too. Though no one yet dared propose it, everyone understood the logical extension. Global net coverage. The end of malaria.

CHAPTER 3

The Selfish Philanthropist

It is three days before I visit Apac. We are high above the crater of Ngorongoro in the Serengeti en route from Tanzania to Uganda when Ray Chambers unclips his safety belt and beckons me to follow him to the back of the plane. The UN special envoy for malaria is graying, and his movements are a little stiff, but for sixty-six, he is still trim and square-jawed, his looks complemented by a low Clint Eastwood whisper. Chambers travels like a star too: the plane, the size of a small commercial jet, is his own. At the front, just behind the cockpit, are eight wide leather seats where we have been sitting for takeoff. At the rear are a double bedroom and walk-in closet with neatly pressed shirts, ties, and suits. Over the wings is a lounge—a TV, a drinks cabinet, and two sofas facing each other. Chambers sits on one and indicates I should take the other.

As an assistant serves Coke and pretzels, Chambers starts to talk. His conversation is peppered with casually startling statements like: "So in March of 1987, I decided to kind of adopt

1,000 of the children of Newark." Or: "So after September 11, we kind of began looking at what we could do for world peace."[1] He mentions friends like P. Diddy, Ashton Kutcher, Bono, and Jeffrey Sachs, and meetings with the Dalai Lama and receptions at the White House. From anyone else this might be irritating. But Chambers, I realize, is not showing off. People with private planes just fly a little higher than the rest of us.

Chambers's origins were humble. He was born and raised in the poor, depressed East Coast immigrant port city of Newark, New Jersey, the son of a warehouse manager. He put himself through an accounting degree at Rutgers University by singing and playing piano for a rock 'n' roll cover band, the Raytones— a past that explains the enduring rockabilly hint to his hair. His first job was as a tax accountant at the Newark branch of Price Waterhouse.

By 1968, at just twenty-five, Chambers felt he was ready to branch out on his own. He bought into a nursing home company called Metrocare Enterprises and installed himself as chair and president. He made his first million dollars when he took Metrocare public in 1969 and stayed for another seven years, steadily expanding and acquiring other businesses. In 1975, he quit.

In later decades, those seven years in one job would seem uncharacteristic of a man who, perhaps more than anyone, came to personify the get-rich-quick spirit of the 1980s. But the 1970s were a time of recession and fear, when banking and accountancy were staid, clubby professions for men who liked golf and a long lunch. Chambers had some radical ideas about how to change banks and finance. But they were fraught with risk, experimentation was discouraged in a downturn, and he was young, with no track record in the industry. In later years, bankers would come to see that profile not as a disqualification but as an attribute. But with times as they were, Chambers had to be patient.

In 1975, his frustration boiled over. He left Metrocare and used his savings to buy a series of small, soundly managed companies with low debt. Chambers's first insight was to understand that these firms, many of them undervalued by the stock downturn of the 1970s, could support far higher debt. His second was to realize that debt was the best way to get rich without already being so. If he borrowed against the value of the company he was about to buy—putting up the company as collateral, in the same way as a house is used to support a mortgage—he could buy into companies far beyond the reach of his own resources. If he borrowed heavily enough, he could buy a controlling position. When the company's value rose, as it should with an undervalued company under Chambers's aggressive management, he would sell off his shares, pay back the debt, and keep the difference. If prices rose high enough, he could make a killing. For a stake of a few thousand dollars and a few months' interest payments, he'd be taking all the profit, potentially in the millions.

Though the term had yet to be coined, Chambers had imagined the leveraged buyout—a concept that, once his competitors figured out what he was doing, would dominate business and finance in the 1980s. Leverage would spark a wave of mergers and takeovers and, with the instant fortunes it created, define the mood and culture of the times. Investment changed its meaning, from something you put a little into to get a little out of to something you put very little into to get a whole lot out of. Investment banking became less about careful research than out-and-out gambling. Ivy League types in the venerable investment houses on Wall Street were replaced by young Turks from city colleges. Across the Atlantic, the City of London changed from a square mile of establishment banks staffed by men in bowler hats to a mecca for Porsche-driving chancers from the East End.

Chambers was among the first of this new breed. In 1981, already a leverage veteran at age thirty-nine, he formed an investment house with William Simon, fifteen years his senior, who had briefly served as Richard Nixon's treasury secretary. With Chambers's acumen and Simon's contacts, the pair "kind of kicked off the whole leveraged buy-out movement," says Chambers. Their first acquisition, in 1980, was an oyster farm. In September 1981, they formalized their partnership in an investment firm they christened Wesray after Simon's initials and Chambers's first name. In January 1982, in a deal still studied in business schools today, Wesray bought Gibson Greetings, the third-largest maker of greeting cards in the US. The deal was breathtaking in its audacity. Chambers, Simon, and a third partner put up $333,000 each. They paid the balance of $80.5 million by selling some of Gibson's assets and mortgaging others. Gibson flourished, and its shares rose. Wesray began selling off its stock in mid-1983. Eventually, the three partners made a $70 million profit each—a return of more than two hundred times their original stakes. In 1985, Chambers topped even that. Using just $10 million of Wesray's capital, by then $408 million, and borrowing the balance, Chambers bought the giant car rental company Avis for $1 billion—then sold it fourteen months later for $1.75 billion to an employee stock ownership plan, a profit of $740 million. In 1988, *Forbes* magazine estimated Chambers's personal wealth at more than $200 million. It has multiplied many times since. "We had a great deal of luck," says Chambers.[2]

Today Chambers is reluctant to talk about the old days. That may stem from a surprising realization that dawned on him even as the millions rolled in: money didn't make him happy. "In 1985, Bill Simon came into my office and said: 'Isn't this great?'" says Chambers. "'But you don't look happy. What would it take to make you happy?' And I said: 'If we lost it all, we could do it all over again.' But more and more, I began to realize that increasing your wealth was not going to make you feel more contented, and that that was not making great use of your life on earth."

Chambers began hanging out in a destitute area of Newark at a project for poor inner-city teenagers, mostly blacks, mostly living with single mothers. He became, as he says, "engaged in the lives of these kids" in a way that he had rarely felt in his life. Which is how in March 1987, Chambers came to promise one thousand of them that he would pay their tuition through college "if they stayed the path." Chambers's involvement only deepened after that. "I found myself not wanting to go back to the office. Eventually I said: 'Fellas, let's take a year to figure out what to do with Wesray. And if we don't come up with anything, let's close it.' And in June 1989, we closed Wesray, and I put all my assets in trust."

Over the next four years, Chambers would give away around $50 million, according to an estimate at the time by the *New York Times*. The year he closed Wesray, he set up the Amelior Foundation to channel his money. At first, Chambers's cash went only to Newark. He made grants to the Boys & Girls Clubs of Newark. He helped fund a new $190 million New Jersey Performing Arts Center. He also helped buy, for $150 million, a basketball team, the New Jersey Nets, and install it in a new arena in a deprived area of the city. He put money toward Newark's first movie theater. "He was the first Newark boy who really put his money on the line and made it happen," says Barton Myers, architect of the new art center. "No one would have thought you could raise $190 million in Newark and build an arts center."[3] Chambers's prominence in the wider charity world also rose. In 1991, with the backing and funding of then president George Bush, he formed the Points of Light Foundation, a program for successful professionals to mentor underprivileged children that would eventually grow to include five million mentors.

For all his beneficence, the world didn't hear much about Ray Chambers, and for one good reason: he wanted it that way. "Ray is the only example I know of someone keeping a PR firm on retainer to make sure he stayed *out* of the press," says Suprotik Basu, later to become a key aide to Chambers in the UN special envoy's office.[4] In 1992 Chambers did agree to an interview with the *Wall Street Journal* but only if the reporter first performed five months of community service, and even then Chambers only communicated by fax.

Chambers had his reasons for staying in the shadows. He discovered that, personally, he didn't need the approval of others to make him feel good. For him, giving was its own reward. Chambers had reached that conclusion after lengthy research. Curious about his own transformation from accumulator to philanthropist, he responded as he always had when confronted by a puzzle: he crunched data. Chambers began gathering material on giving and philanthropy wherever he could find it, moving from scientific journals and religious teachings to pieces of consumer research. "Saatchi & Saatchi did a psychological probe to understand why people gave," he says. "And they discovered that right after we are born, when our mothers first leave us, we experience what's known as a narcissistic injury. All our lives we try to cope with [this]. And nothing fills the hole better than engaging in the life of somebody less fortunate."

Chambers also explored more ethereal arenas. He visited the Californian spiritualist Deepak Chopra, "who teaches from the Vedas ways to get to a new self, soul and God, and that one of the most efficient ways to do that is to help somebody less fortunate—and that whether the person thanks you or not, it doesn't matter." He took in some Tibetan Buddhism too. "Five years ago, I saw the Dalai Lama in New York. They were doing these CAT scans of Tibetan monks who had meditated on kindness and compassion. And they compared them, the colors on them, which parts were most active, to other brains. A Tibetan monk has a completely different brain from the brain of a CEO." One monk, Matthieu Ricard, a Frenchman who gave up a career in science to study Buddhism in the Himalayas, made a particular impression. "He came over to my apartment, and as he walked in, the apartment just lit up," says Chambers. "Within five minutes, you knew you were in the presence of the happiest man that ever lived."

Ricard taught Chambers two things. First, "happiness comes from oneself only." Second, "the shortest route toward happiness is in the service of others." Taken together, that added up to a paradox. To be happy, Chambers didn't need anyone's help. But he did need others *to* help. Just as contradictory, while Chambers's new path was to be in the service of others, it was underwritten by self-interest. Even if he was helping others, he was still pursuing his own happiness—only that no longer depended on "gathering acorns and treasures for oneself. It's about putting others before you." Chambers, leverage king, Wall Street wizard, had discovered enlightened self-interest. It was in his best interest, it turned out, to be good to others.

Why make money only to give it away? Philanthropy can be about selfless duty, and Chambers had a well-developed conscience.

"I had never seen people as down-and-out as the people of [1980s] Newark," he told the *Wall Street Journal* in 1992. "It had gotten so bad I didn't think I had any alternative."[5] But philanthropy can also be about feeling good—something that not only sustained Chambers on the new path he had created for himself but helped him sell it to others. In meetings in the boardrooms and homes of America's wealthy and famous, Chambers told his audiences this was still about getting ahead, still about being number one, still about serving yourself. Only now it was about accumulating staggering great sacks of spiritual satisfaction.

Chambers had solved the paradox of millionaire philanthropy. Making a pile and then giving it all away was not a contradiction. By Chambers's reasoning, it was almost logical: you *had* to make money to give it all away, and doing that was actually the most selfishly fulfilling thing in the world. By this view, self-interest and altruism actually ran side by side. It was the element of altruism that made philanthropy admirable, but it was the element of self-interest that ensured it was enduring and efficient. Conscience was dropping a bill in the poor box once a year; self-interest was setting up your own foundation and monitoring how your money was spent.

And if Chambers was bringing the mind-set of an entrepreneur to philanthropy, he was also borrowing the techniques. He ran Amelior like a business. He established a nonprofit commodities-trading fund to raise cash. He networked to find investors in his social projects just as he would for his commercial ones. He made himself a kind of charity-world CEO, accountable to his funders for a project's success. He calculated his and others' performance by business measurements such as return on capital and ability to meet deadlines. "Ray approaches social issues like a CEO approaches a company," says Basu. "He breaks it down into supply chains, investment decisions, sales and marketing, accountancy."

Crucially, Chambers also deployed his secret weapon for getting more from less—leverage. His approach had three pillars: political leadership, business leadership, and the media. Playing them off against each other to multiply their effect was Chambers's peculiar skill. Steven Phillips of ExxonMobil, also an advisor in years to come, calls it "the Ray Chambers model for development and saving the world." "Everything Ray went on to do in malaria was built on what he did in Newark," says Phillips. "He was a skillful leader with an intense understanding of the levers of power. He knew how to change institutions for the benefit of mankind. He knew how to change the world."[6]

The system worked, says Phillips, as "a triangle of leverage and accountability." "Ray would go to business and say, 'With my money, I will help elect an effective mayor, the kind of mayor that you deserve. But in return, you need to invest in X, Y, and Z—and I will coinvest with you.' Then after fixing the politics and attracting local business interest, he would invite the media in to do these snapshot profiles about the new breed of Newark politician and business leader who were revitalizing the city. It appealed to their vanity. But it was also an accountability tool: now they'd committed to rebuilding Newark in public. It was brilliant, really brilliant. And it really worked."

Here too was another reason for staying in the background. The Newark model for social change left Chambers no room for personal publicity. How would allowing himself to be congratulated in public endear Chambers to his peers or persuade them to part with their money? Far better to let them take the credit. Credit, of any kind, was the currency of leverage.

From the map display on Chambers's plane, I can see we are leaving the Serengeti, passing north over the Mara River and into Kenya. It is August, the summer rains are over, and the landscape is brown and parched. Below us, in the eastern Rift Valley, more than a million wildebeest and zebras who have followed the rains north will be turning south once more on their never-ending quest for greener grass. As we watch the great plains pass beneath us, Chambers recounts how it was there in January 2006 that his interest in malaria began to solidify.

By that time, Chambers had been giving his money to good causes for more than fifteen years, but his efforts were still largely confined to the US. In the aftermath of 9/11, it dawned on him that the same anger he had seen on the streets of Newark— a destructive frustration at deprivation and exclusion—was also fueling Muslim radicals around the world. Inequality provides the incentives to make capitalism work. But if that disparity is made insurmountable by barriers like poverty, poor education, corruption, class, or caste, then the incentive becomes one not to legitimate advancement but advancement by any means necessary. Islamists felt the US unfairly dominated world politics, economics, religion, and culture. The 9/11 attacks were the ultimate expression of the fury that inequality could produce and the clearest demonstration of why it was in all our interests to do something about it—in this case, less for our own satisfaction than to prevent war.[7] "The root of the problem was this animosity," says Chambers. "In February 2002, [then secretary of state] Colin Powell spoke to the World Economic Forum and basically said: 'We will never have peace unless we level the playing field.' So with my family and the staff at the foundation, we kind of began trying to figure out what we could do to do that."

Initially, Chambers hit upon the idea of an interfaith conference, bringing together all the world's religious leaders—
Christian, Muslim, Jews, the Dalai Lama—and asking them to
appeal to all their followers to lay down their arms, at least for
the three to four days of the meeting. After months of negotiations and discussions with faith groups around the world, "we
concluded it was a great idea," says Chambers, "but perhaps
not doable."

After that, says Chambers, "we were kind of groping around"
when a friend briefed him on the Millennium Development Goals
(MDGs), the eight minimum standards of poverty alleviation and
health that, at the turn of the new millennium, 192 members of
the United Nations had vowed to make universal by 2015. The
eight goals were:

1. Halve poverty and hunger.
2. Ensure universal primary education for all.
3. Ensure gender equality at all education levels.
4. Cut child mortality by two-thirds.
5. Cut maternal mortality by three-quarters; ensure all mothers can access reproductive health services.
6. Halt and start to reverse the spread of HIV/AIDS and ensure universal treatment for those infected; halt and start
   to reverse malaria.
7. Promote environmental sustainability, protect biodiversity,
   halve numbers without access to safe drinking water, and
   significantly improve the lives of a hundred million slum
   dwellers.
8. Develop a global partnership for development that includes
   an open and fair international financial system, cooperat-
   ing with drug companies and other private businesses to

provide drugs and technology to the poor, ease debt, and focus aid on the poorest countries.[8]

Chambers's first reaction was: "These are so daunting. These are so unlikely to be achieved." But his friend left Chambers a card with the MDGs printed on them, and when he looked at them again, Chambers saw signs of something else. Foreign aid was, traditionally, almost the opposite of business—a selfless promise of help, with the emphasis more on intentions than results. But the MDGs contained a limited number of set goals and included a deadline. They were, in effect, a rudimentary business plan. "I began to think: 'Well, at least these are quantifiable, at least they're measurable. And a hundred-ninety-something nations have agreed to them.'" There was a looseness to the language and wide scope for interpretation. But maybe, thought Chambers, aid was changing.

As ever, Chambers began gathering data on this new issue. He read through the academic literature on the macroeconomics of health and quickly came across Jeffrey Sachs. "It was clear that Sachs was the originator of the MDGs, so I had some mutual friends introduce us, and I went to visit him at his office at Columbia University. And I loved his intelligence, his energy, his positivity. So I started coming back, and we had a series of meetings over about six months." Chambers would drill Sachs for information and answers. Sachs, well practiced in his arguments and ready with a thousand examples, became Chambers's guide through the nuances of global poverty and development—and would challenge Chambers, with all his skills and resources, to do something about it.

Chambers could have had no more evangelical teacher than Sachs. Like Chambers, Sachs had performed something of a midlife reversal. In the 1980s and 1990s, he advised several developing countries, including Bolivia and Poland, on how to implement shock therapy—the rapid implementation of free market reform in economies moving from socialism to capitalism. As Sachs intended, inflation fell, and inefficient, bureaucratic state enterprises either reformed or failed. But incomes also crashed, and unemployment and inequality rose. To his consternation, Sachs found he was making as many enemies as friends in the developing world.

Thereafter, Sachs reinvented himself as a champion of the poor. He campaigned loudly for rapid acceleration of aid. He was outspoken about the need to cancel Third World debt. In 2002, the then UN secretary-general, Kofi Annan, appointed him to a new post working out how the world might achieve the MDGs. As a result, Sachs found himself becoming that rarity in the staid profession of economics: a leading expert on the developing world, something close to a celebrity, sought after by governments, billionaires, and Hollywood actors interested in fighting poverty but unsure how to go about it.

Under Sachs's tutelage, Chambers soon found he was "looking for a business plan to achieve the MDGs, because I didn't see anything that was simple and direct enough." His opinion hardened when another friend, Charles McCormack, the CEO of Save the Children USA, told Chambers the various organizations trying to meet the MDGs were a "bunch of musicians playing their tunes, but we don't have a conductor to bring us all together." "So," says Chambers, "Jeff and I kind of formed Millennium Promise to bring them together."

As he navigated this new world, Chambers began noticing that one issue came up time and again: malaria. Of the eight MDGs, at least three—MDG 6, but also MDGs 4 and 5—could be said to apply to malaria, and possibly MDG 1 as well.

Sachs had also zeroed in on the disease. In his seminal book *The End of Poverty*, Sachs argued the poorest countries were locked in a poverty trap from which only aid could rescue them. He added that, given advances in medicine and the world's long experience of how to engineer development, doing that was no longer difficult if only donors had the will. If we did, Sachs claimed extreme poverty—living on $1 or less a day—would be history in twenty years.

Malaria, said Sachs, was a great place to start. The disease was a test of development: each country's ability to cope with it was a good way to rank its advancement. But did Africa have malaria because it was poor? Or was it that malaria was keeping Africa poor? Sachs said it was both. "Africa's governance is poor because Africa is poor," he wrote. Later he calculated malaria cost Africa $12 billion a year in lost output. This, said Sachs, was a downward spiral, and a big reason Africa seemed locked in poverty.

By the same reasoning, fixing malaria would have exponential benefits. It would save lives. And the process of fixing it—of executing a policy and assessing the results—would also improve systems of government. A malaria-free country, whose victory over the disease had required a better government, would develop more quickly. A more developed country would feed back again into an even more capable state directing its people to further prosperity. In 2000, when he was at Harvard, Sachs conducted a study that found a 10 percent reduction in malaria cases would raise economic growth by 0.3 percent a year.[9] This was an upward spiral. It was Africa's path out of poverty. What's more, wrote Sachs, it was a good deal. Fixing it would take $3 billion a year, a quarter of its annual cost to Africa's economy.

Sachs's arguments made sense to the businessman in Chambers. Fixing malaria was like an investment: it would improve a country's capabilities and move it out of poverty toward optimism and growth. Chambers also knew that business had much to teach the aid world about efficiency. The pursuit of personal profit may have helped produce the inequality of the 1980s—when billionaires coexisted with the homeless (in the West) and the starving (in Africa and Asia)—that made aid necessary. But Chambers contended that was not, as many aid workers believed, an argument for dispensing with business methods in aid—rather, it was a case for putting such tools to work in aid as well. And here, malaria was an issue that cried out for the right kind of foreign aid—urgent, efficient, not a handout, but a temporary boost to speed a nation toward the day it was able to care for itself.

The issue of malaria also appealed to Chambers's ideas of enlightened self-interest. Malaria didn't continue to exist because we couldn't fix it. Ways of curing it had been known for centuries, and preventing it for decades. Malaria had not been fixed, Chambers realized, because the rich world chose not to. That was the narrow logic of Chambers's previous incarnation as a winner-takes-all Wall Street titan. Now Chambers believed the rich world should help the poor world in its own interest. It wasn't so much that inequality was unjustifiable—though extreme disparity clearly was. It was that inequality was unintelligent. Poverty didn't just hurt the poor. It hurt everyone. A malaria-free Africa would cost the West less in assistance and benefit it more as a trading partner, just as surely as a world in which young Muslims felt less oppressed would be one of fewer terrorist attacks.

Chambers set up a series of meetings with malaria specialists at places like the US Centers for Disease Control and Prevention and the World Health Organization. One person he met was Steven Phillips, an occupational medicine expert at ExxonMobil. "My advice was: 'We need your leadership,'" says Phillips. "'We've got to make the international architecture of the various groups dealing with malaria more effective, as they don't play ball together. We have to vastly ramp up resources. And we have to get African leaders on board, or none of this will be sustainable.' Ray knew almost nothing about malaria at the time. But he was a quick study, and within six months he'd worked up the Ray Chambers Plan for Malaria that basically applied his three-pillar Newark model to the problem. For political leadership, get President Bush and the African Union. For investors, get people like the Global Fund and the World Bank. Then get the media to come along with their flashbulbs and get everyone committing to malaria in public."

The signature project for Chambers's and Sachs's joint foundation, Millennium Promise, was the Millennium Villages. These were thirteen showcase African villages chosen to host a comprehensive effort to achieve the eight MDGs—to show success was possible and to highlight the benefits. To drum up funding, Sachs and Chambers traveled to Kenya to two of the villages in January 2006 with a small group of potential donors.

Sachs and Chambers were both at pivotal moments in their lives. Sachs was at the height of his influence: he had just finished his report for Annan and in December had published *The End of Poverty*, which, unusually for an academic tome on development, became an instant best seller and was even excerpted as a cover for *Time* magazine. Chambers, meanwhile, was seeing malaria for himself for the first time. The experience was powerful confirmation of his view that malaria was, as Basu says, "a no-brainer. He couldn't think of a reason why the world should not go to work on malaria. He was moved by the suffering, of course, but also by how fixable it was."

After Kenya, Chambers and Sachs split up. Chambers went on to Uganda. Sachs flew to Malawi and Mozambique to visit other Millennium Villages. A few weeks later, the pair reunited in New York to compare experiences and photographs. "Jeff has this one picture of a room of angelic children, all sleeping," says Chambers. "And I say, 'Ah, aren't they cute?' But Jeff says: 'Ray, you don't understand. They're all in malarious comas. They're all dying.' And they did all die." Chambers was mortified. But suddenly he knew. "So I said to Jeff: 'I'd like to kind of come up with some business concepts to see if we can't save a million children a year.'"

CHAPTER 4

Aiding Who?

There were already hundreds of thousands of people trying to figure out how to save a million children a year, not least their parents. And there were good reasons to think it might be impossible. One was the collapse of the previous campaign. A second, and one of rising significance, was the more generalized failings of all aid, and the increasing criticism to which it was subjected. Covering the 2008–2009 economic crisis, I received a valuable lesson in why foreign assistance was increasingly under fire.

By the end of 2008, the world's leading aid and development professionals were warning, in an endless stream of speeches and press releases, that the gathering economic crisis would be most damaging to the poor. Through 2009 and 2010, as the depression spread from finance to the real economy, they united in a siren warning: the world was getting poorer, and, for the poorest of the poor, that would mean disaster. The downturn would push tens of millions of people into poverty. It would gut donations. Famines and mass migrations were imminent.

For a journalist, this was a compellingly tragic narrative. Not only were the poorest least able to cope, with a crisis that originated in the rich world they were also least to blame. For months, leaders of the aid world used their authority to make sure the story got out. In an address to a special session of the UN Human Rights Council in February 2009, UN High Commissioner for Human Rights Navi Pillay said economic decline was likely to "undermine access to work, affordability of food and housing, as well as of water, basic health care and education" and identified "women and children, migrants, refugees, indigenous peoples, minorities and persons with disabilities" as "at the frontlines of hardship . . . and most likely to lose their jobs and access to social safety nets and services."[1] In April, Joy Phumaphi, then vice president for human development at the World Bank, claimed the slump had "taken a wrecking ball to growth and development in the developing world, with children having to drop out of school and poor families eating cheaper, less nutritious food which can result in weight loss and severe malnutrition."[2] The same month World Bank president Robert Zoellick warned of the "human catastrophe" of what he said were fifty-five million to ninety million people then being pushed into poverty, which the Bank measures as a daily income of $1.25 or less.[3] As the world's poorest continent, Africa was a focus of concern. The World Bank's managing director, former finance minister of Nigeria Ngozi Okonjo-Iweala, said the crisis would thrust forty-six million Africans into absolute poverty. International Monetary Fund (IMF) chief Dominique Strauss-Kahn went further. "This is not only about protecting economic growth and household incomes," he said. "It is also about containing the threat of civil unrest, perhaps even war."[4]

None of this happened. There was no rise in poverty. The downturn caused no wars and no unrest. Africa not only weathered the recession far better than much of the world but actually got richer. Only South Africa, the continent's richest country, went briefly into recession. The other forty-seven countries in sub-Saharan Africa kept growing by an average 5.6 percent in 2008, 2 percent in 2009, 5 percent in 2010, returning to a predicted 5.5 percent in 2011.[5] Least affected by the downturn were the poorest countries. Africa's twenty-nine low-income countries grew by a healthy 4.5 percent in 2009, when the recession's impact on the rest of the world was at its highest. And contrary to predictions of slashed aid budgets, assistance rose too. Total global aid went up by 6.8 percent to $119.6 billion in 2009. In 2010, when the US and Britain ring-fenced foreign aid even as they trimmed and slashed spending in almost every other area, it increased again, by another 5 percent to $126 billion.[6] In Africa, the focus of much of the concern, aid rose by 3 percent to $27 billion. Spending on health and education in Africa also went up.[7]

I was among a number of journalists who began asking whether they'd been deceived. And in April 2010, the IMF's director for Africa, Antoinette Sayeh, did admit the predictions of catastrophe had been flat wrong. "Somewhat surprisingly to some, many of the region's low-income countries appear to have been less affected," she said. "[They] escaped fairly lightly in terms of the impact of the crisis. Low-income countries were able then to sustain their growth. In fact, several of the fragile countries were able to accelerate output in 2009."[8]

Mistakes can be forgiven if they are innocent or well intentioned, as Sayeh implied. But a little investigation revealed these were neither. The aid world, I discovered, knew by mid-2009 the crisis would barely affect Africa. The truth was contained in its own figures. By June 2009, World Bank managing director Okonjo-Iweala was scaling back her statistics. No longer were forty-six million Africans being pushed into poverty, she said. Now, she told the World Economic Forum on Africa in Cape Town, the figure was more like six million. Likewise, despite Strauss-Kahn's rhetoric, the IMF was forecasting low-income countries in Africa would grow 4.6 percent in 2009 and fragile countries by 3.1 percent.[9]

But these quiet confessions were the exceptions. In September 2009, the World Bank's Zoellick was still talking up the impending disaster. "The poor and most vulnerable are at greatest risk from economic shocks," he said. "Families are pushed into poverty, health conditions deteriorate, school attendance declines, and progress in other critical areas is stalled or reversed."[10] Aid organizations also maintained the chorus of concern. Ritu Sharma, president of Women Thrive Worldwide, a US-based NGO that campaigns to lift women out of poverty, said: "Many people in developing countries . . . are eating less than they were before."[11] Donations had to rise, said Oxfam America president Ray Offenheiser, and "it is crucial that this is additive and not deducted from current aid budgets."[12]

I found it hard not to conclude that the aid world, or part of it, sees crisis as opportunity. That, after all, is the dynamic of aid. A crisis occurs. Aid agencies ask for money to fix it. And this is how it should be, with two provisos, the first of which is if the crisis is real. And second, if the aid agencies actually fix it.

Most aid workers are conscientious, well-motivated people prepared to endure some rough living. As individuals, their sincerity is rarely in question and the horrors they can witness beyond doubt. They have achieved some unquestioned triumphs, particularly fighting disease. The eradication of smallpox. The near eradication of polio. Successful battles against epidemics of syphilis, measles, tetanus, flu, and iodine deficiency. The mass treatment in the 1950s of the tropical skin and bone infection yaws—barely remembered today but at the time an affliction for fifty million to a hundred million people around the world. They've had success outside medicine too. The feeding of tens of millions. The education of tens of millions more. The financing of vital infrastructure such as roads, waterways, and airports. The preservation of some of the world's oldest artifacts and monuments.

Anyone contemplating a global war on malaria would want to replicate those successes. But aid's critics are voicing increasing doubts about whether aid agencies tell the truth not just about the need but also about how helpful they actually are. For all aid workers' good intentions and past achievements, aid can be terrible value for money. In 2002, basing his calculations on the World Bank's own figures, New York University professor of economics William Easterly discovered it took $3,521 in aid to raise a single poor person's income by $3.65 a year.[13] Many others have noted that countries that receive aid often don't develop. Despite hundreds of billions of dollars in donations, the number of Africans living on less than $1 a day doubled between 1981 and 2001, from 164 million to 316 million.[14] Aid agencies counter that because you find aid in poor places doesn't mean that aid causes poverty—rather it shows aid is going to the right places. That has some merit. But with each passing year, if places receiving aid continue to have little to show for it, it has less and less.

Ineffectiveness bankrupts the case for aid. Aid is, in effect, a censure of a foreign government. It says you are doing an unacceptably poor job. We, the world, can and must do better. But if aid can't or doesn't do better, then the argument falls apart. Ineffective aid is unjustifiable aid. And aid's frequent failures bolster the view, common among African governments, that it is little more than Western arrogance in a white SUV.

And if the problem is ineffectiveness, the cause, very often, is aid's ambiguous position: a profession that is increasingly a business but that operates outside normal commercial strictures. Aid started simply, as compassion. But it has grown into a giant industry of tens of thousands of nongovernmental organizations together worth an annual $120 billion[15]—about the same as the annual output of the twenty poorest of the forty-eight countries in sub-Saharan Africa. Aid workers today plot well-rewarded careers from African village projects through to aid agency regional headquarters and on to the UN in New York or Switzerland. Aid agencies operate increasingly like competing businesses: advertising, submitting bids for aid contracts, exploring opportunities for expansion. The UN even has its own airline, running to two hundred to two hundred fifty aircraft for its peacekeeping operations alone.

But aid's transformation from benevolence to business has been incomplete, and that creates problems. In some ways, these are unavoidable because of aid's peculiar nature. One immutable difference between aid and business, for instance, is that aid is paid for by people who do not receive it. That is generous, no doubt. But at a stroke it also erases consumer rights: aid's recipients have little say in what they receive and no interest in what it costs.

The distance between product and consumer is reflected in other awkward ways. When businesses export, they do so through satellite operations in importing countries whose primary job is to integrate the product into the local market—to shed its foreignness—as much as possible. Aid is exclusively an export business. But its satellite operations are almost always run by expatriates on short-run contracts whose level of integration is more akin to the foreign diplomats they so closely resemble.

Distance also means that while aid agencies are theoretically subject to the same public scrutiny and advertising regulations that govern business, they rarely are in practice. The separation—by thousands of miles and poor communication—of a project from its funders or an advertising campaign from the place it depicts means it is hard to call out an aid agency—or even the entire aid industry—when it misleads you by, say, talking up a nonexistent emergency.

Some of the differences between aid and business are less nature than nurture, however. A good business should never die. But a good aid agency always should, since the ultimate goal of any aid project should be the day it is no longer needed. In practice, that turns out to be a principle nearly all aid agencies are happy to ignore.

Similarly, many aid groups reject as inappropriate, even offensive, standard business tools for measuring performance such as return on investment, deadlines, and cost-benefit analysis. Aid workers' pursuit of social improvement and disdain for personal profit can make that seem like an admirable personal choice, and often it is. Their use of rules and guidelines as substitutes also has its merits: aid needs regulation as much as business does. But removing the discipline of the market can have damaging effects. As Chambers understood, the inequalities created by the pursuit of profit are not, as many aid workers believe, an argument for discarding business methods—rather they are an argument for applying those methods to aid to achieve similar success. Not using performance assessments allows aid agencies to sidestep many of the normal checks on business behavior and leaves adherence to regulations an agency's only measure of its success.

And staying within the law tells you nothing about real achievement, only that minimum standards have been met. Moreover, strict regulation can usher in an inflexibility that makes it hard to adjust to conditions on the ground.

These structural conundrums, these missing incentives, can sound academic, even obscure. My work as a correspondent in Africa revealed them as anything but. On reporting trips across the continent, I found a highly bureaucratic trade had evolved, managed by a confusing army of actors who might be international or national, independent or state, giant or tiny—a situation that inevitably led to waste. And because it was rarely measured, performance was often poor. I saw the wrong aid arrive in the wrong place, or late, or costing too much. Again and again I saw money spent on fleets of cars and ranks of furnished offices and villas rather than actual assistance—until the mere sight of a white Toyota Land Cruiser was enough to spark an instant surge of anger. Little of any of this was assessed. The results of some projects were never measured, and few were compared for their relative returns.

A business that consistently delivers subpar results, or misses deadlines, or cannot account for money spent will eventually go bust or at least stop winning tenders. Not so in aid, where good projects were trumpeted but bad ones, I learned, merely downplayed. Individuals were rarely judged by performance. Failure was sad, but it didn't cost anyone their job. Aid was often ineffective simply because efficiency was not the priority.

Worryingly for those proposing a global malaria campaign, these problems were bigger inside the larger agencies. Businesses, driven by the need to carve out a niche in the market, focus on different sectors. Likewise, there were hundreds of smaller aid agencies in Africa and Asia concentrating on one area or a particular type of relief—specialized groups that were often the most effective.

But the more established agencies found that since no one measured their performance or judged where their skills lay, they didn't have to specialize. Far from folding once an aid project was completed, they did the opposite: expand in every possible direction. The core proposition of today's aid Goliaths—the various UN humanitarian agencies, as well as Oxfam, Care, Goal, World Vision, and so on—is an indiscriminate offer of help: in one country they might be digging wells, in another running a school, in a third distributing medicine, in a fourth advising on microfinance. They bid for a project not so much because they are expert in it—they might be, they might not—but because that is where the money is. What specialization occurs is so minor as to be all but meaningless. UNICEF and Save the Children confine themselves to the world's youth. The WHO restricts itself to global health.

For anyone contemplating a global war on malaria, the big agencies would be essential. But from observing them across Africa, I had gathered plenty of real-life warnings about the pitfalls of big aid. Southern Sudan was one example of how inefficiency explained why some countries that attracted the most aid also continued to be the poorest. In 2005, the international community set up a $526 million Southern Sudan Multi-Donor Trust Fund administered by the World Bank to pay for roads, running water, agriculture, health, and education for eight million to nine million southern Sudanese. The south was due to secede from the north in a referendum in 2011, and, with almost none of the institutions, infrastructure, or economy that would normally define an independent country, there was an urgent need to build at least the skeleton of a nation. I visited in February 2010 with the vote on independence less than a year away. A high-level World Bank delegation was also there to investigate why there had been so little development in the past five years and in particular why its staff had dispersed only $217 million of the Fund. One key reason: the southern Sudanese initially had no bank account into which the Bank could pay the money, and it had taken an entire year before a World Bank representative flew to Nairobi with a counterpart from the southern Sudan authorities to show him how to open one.

Ethiopia illustrated another type of big aid ineffectiveness: how helping a country can cripple its ability to help itself and even institutionalize crisis. In 2008, I spent weeks reporting a giant famine in East Africa, watching food aid being handed out at feeding centers from Tanzania through Kenya and Somalia to Ethiopia, an emergency that took in close to twenty million people. Bizarrely, at the center of the disaster, southern Ethiopia, the hills were green, the livestock healthy, and the fields freshly plowed. This was hunger caused not by a natural disaster but by humans. While decades of Western food aid had stopped people from going hungry in the short term, in the long term it ensured they did: free food undercut and ruined African farmers, who were not working on a charitable basis but a commercial one.[16]

Humanitarian aid operations in response to natural disasters— like the 2004–2005 Asian tsunami, the earthquakes in Kashmir in 2005 and Haiti in 2010, or the 2010 floods in Pakistan— illustrate a similar phenomenon. Disasters require a humanitarian response, no doubt. But the provision of food, blankets, and shelter can only ever mitigate a crisis in the short term, not solve it in the long term. That requires a country—or more specifically its government—to raise its ability to look after its own. But governments that never learn those skills because they are sidelined by foreign aid agencies risk being forever dependent on handouts. After the tsunami and the Kashmir earthquake, foreign humanitarians managed to put millions of people into tents, but no one—not they, not the government—had a plan to get them out again. Likewise in Haiti, 1.5 million were still living under canvas ten months after the earthquake there when the first outbreak of cholera hit.

Tending to human suffering in response to human-made disasters—war, ethnic cleansing, a coup, a dictatorship—but ignoring their political causes can also mean the problem is never solved because it is never addressed. Humanitarian operations can even make the situation worse. In Darfur, the militants who prompted the exodus of two million refugees hid out, regrouped, and recruited in foreign-funded feeding camps before heading back out to continue fighting. They knew aid workers, sworn to the humanitarian's code of neutrality, wouldn't refuse them. Likewise in eastern DRC, after the 1994 genocide in neighboring Rwanda, humanitarian aid workers fed and clothed the Hutu militants who had killed eight hundred thousand Rwandans before fleeing over the border. Philip Gourevitch, chronicler of the genocide, describes that as not so much fixing the crisis as "catering it."

To anyone who has ever visited a refugee camp, the confused incentives of modern aid are manifested memorably in another practice the agencies have borrowed from business without the attendant accountability: branding. Humanitarian aid groups have taken to hoisting giant flags over displacement centers, clothing refugees in T-shirts emblazoned with logos, and flying more flags from their Land Cruisers. Once this was about indicating neutrality. Today it is just as symptomatic of an industry that does not have to deliver results. What, in the end, is the incentive to fix a crisis when managing it *is* the business? Far more important to underline your ownership rights to the situation by branding it.

A global malaria campaign would have to overcome these flaws if it was to work. Of even bigger concern was the failing that had sullied aid's name more than anything else: corruption.

As well as being misused or poorly spent, aid money goes missing. Montek Ahluwalia of India's Planning Commission reckons corruption is so bad in India that only 16 percent of the money intended for the poor under the country's food distribution scheme actually reaches them.[17] Drugs were a commodity especially prone to theft. In Uganda in 1999, 73 percent of all drugs in the public health system were stolen by health administrators and sold privately.[18] And as every aid worker knows, public outrage at corruption is capable of halting entire aid efforts in their tracks. A year after the Asian tsunami of 2004, the Aceh Anti-Corruption Movement calculated 30–40 percent of all the $4.5 billion in aid received by Indonesia was tainted by corruption. Oxfam and Save the Children both suspended operations in the country when the movement revealed the two agencies had employed builders who erected substandard houses or simply disappeared.[19]

Aid workers' behavior can encourage such corruption. The new four-wheel drive cars, housing allowances, tax-free salaries, and workshops in faraway five-star resorts that are the staple of a career in foreign aid may not cost more than what is spent on actual assistance. But flashy cars, big houses, and all-expenses-paid foreign trips are the most visible part of aid— and unsurprisingly this fosters the widespread belief in the developing world that aid is corrupt.

And in a sense, it is. Aid workers raise money by highlighting the conditions of the world's poorest. Then they use millions from that pot to fund their own first-world lifestyles. If you combine a UN salary—in January 2011, wages ranged from $48,627 to $143,929 for a staffer and from $139,074 to $204,391 for a manager—with cost of living and hardship adjustments, a $75,000 car, several thousand dollars a month in rent or hotels, tens of thousands of dollars once a year in business-class flights home for all the family, children's school fees, and tens of thousands more dollars on expenses (satellite phones, health insurance, flying to meetings in Geneva or New York, or conferences across the region), a mid-ranking UN worker can easily burn through half a million dollars a year.[20] Those tempted to defend that in the name of being able to recruit the best should remember that President Barack Obama earns something similar—a salary of $400,000 a year plus $169,000 for travel and other expenses—while at $226,575, British prime minister David Cameron is paid far less. To see the consequences of paying such high wages on painful display, a trip to Goma, eastern DRC, a long-established aid agency base, is instructive. There, wood-shack stores stock Congolese staples—rice, salt, sugar, manioc— and three types of extra virgin olive oil. Refugees get by on staples in the camps while, come evening, expat aid workers choose between low-lit restaurants serving pizza, Mexican, and French along Goma's main drag. Almost all the graceful villas along the shore of Lake Kivu are rented, for thousands of dollars a month, by aid groups. One Sunday in late 2008, I returned to Goma after a week watching the Congolese army rape and murder its way through the hills to the north to witness a group of aid workers water-skiing on the lake behind a scarlet speedboat playing loud rock music, carving out turns in front of the refugees they'd come to help.

The unease surrounding aid is reaching a crescendo. The United Nations is beginning to censure its own. In September 2010,

Radhika Coomaraswamy, UN special representative on children and armed conflict, published a report that examined the construction at the heart of much of modern emergency aid: the refugee camp. Contrary to the widely held belief that underpins the construction of hundreds of tented cities from Colombia to Cambodia, she says that "there was no child more vulnerable in the world" than one in a refugee camp. Children in aid camps face discrimination, are denied documentation or basic rights, and are "at higher risk for becoming victims of grave violations, recruited to be child soldiers [and] at high risk of sexual violence and harassment."[21]

The aid world's usual response to such negative assessments is angry denial. Oxfam released a report in April 2010 that accused much of the "barrage of criticism" of aid of being "incorrect and irresponsible." Drawing a line between "political and ineffective aid" and providers of "good quality, 21st century aid"—Oxfam, presumably—the charity said the case for the latter was "more pressing now than ever." But to illustrate its case, it went on to repeat the same untruths about the recession making the poorest countries poorer. "Last year, the global economic crisis crashed across poor country borders, exacting heavy economic damage and blowing a fiscal hole in the finances of developing countries. Low-income countries—already hit by the prolonged impact of the food and fuel crises—have now seen severe falls in Gross Domestic Product (GDP) growth, resulting in millions more being pushed into poverty."[22]

It's that kind of persistent dissembling that leads aid's harshest critics to declare they don't want to reform the system—they want to tear it down. Among them is William Easterly, who, after he left the World Bank, wrote *The Elusive Quest for Growth* and *The White Man's Burden*, two books that argue aid is often ineffective and frequently damaging. Easterly has become Sachs's nemesis in American academia. The two frequently launch public attacks on each other, and their heated arguments skirt the limits of polite debate. Easterly has now been joined by Zambian former Goldman Sachs banker Dambisa Moyo, whose best-selling 2009 book *Dead Aid* argued assistance should be phased out entirely. In 2010 the Dutch journalist Linda Polman published *War Games*, documenting her experience of aid and the perverse effects it can have. In one agonizing example, Polman uncovers self-congratulation so powerful it leads a group of unqualified Americans to perform surgery on children in West Africa, with predictably lethal results. She also encounters a guerrilla group that admits to carrying out amputations in the hope of drawing more aid.

"I'm sorry to be so unkind to someone who has good intentions," says Easterly, "but you don't get a get-home-free card just for having good intentions. You have to do things that make sense. If a surgeon is about to operate on me, I'm not all that interested in whether he has good intentions. I hope he doesn't have evil intentions, but I'm much more interested in whether he knows what he's doing."[23]

Tellingly, these Western critics find rising support in the developing world. In Africa, aid's most prominent critic is Rwandan president Paul Kagame. "In the last fifty years, you've spent $400 billion in aid to Africa," Kagame told me in an interview in 2007. "The question for our donors is: what difference did it make? What is there to show for it? Obviously somebody's not getting something right. Otherwise, you'd have something to show for your money."

It is that background of rising skepticism to aid that explains the cynicism and pessimism that initially greeted Sachs's proposal to tackle malaria. Aid had already spectacularly failed with malaria once before, and any new plans for elimination or eradication sparked accusations of delusion. For others, piling millions more dollars into an industry whose reputation was increasingly in question was plainly irresponsible.

But encouraged by antipoverty campaigners such as Bono and Bob Geldof, talk of a new campaign against the disease began to circulate in the years around the turn of the millennium. It quickly became apparent, however, that this new initiative would be different.

Next to Sachs, the three people emerging as the key advocates of a fresh drive against malaria were the then world's richest man, Bill Gates, his wife, Melinda, and a Wall Street multimillionaire, Ray Chambers. Not only did none of the three have any expertise in either malaria or public health, these well-funded and well-connected individuals were vowing to merge aid and business as never before. The aid world needed a dose of business discipline, they declared. Campaigns would be run like businesses. Effectiveness and results were the new watchwords.

Disquiet radiated through the aid world. Change was coming, and maybe not for the better. Everything and everyone would henceforth be measured and assessed. More and more, aid agencies would resemble businesses. That was a problem of principle for many. But there was concern about conflicting interests too. Wasn't it business, aid professionals whispered, that for decades had trapped hundreds of millions of Africans in poverty and war?

CHAPTER 5

The Business of Caring

I have a map of Lagos, but from the air I can see it will be useless. The city appears below me as we drop out of the clouds,
and it is endless—a plain of dusty tile and tin roofs extending
all the way to the horizon. Veins of traffic, electric red and
white, glitter prettily in the evening light. Lagos's southern
edge, where I am headed, looks particularly busy: a maze of
skyscrapers jostled against the sea, seemingly squeezing cars
and trucks to a standstill. This is Africa's megacity, the biggest
metropolis in Nigeria, its most populous country and, so the
authorities reckon, soon to be the third largest in the world—
though nobody seems sure whether it is home to 10 or 17.5 or
even 20 million people.[1]

It is December 2009, and in two days I'm meeting Chambers
in Nigeria's inland capital, Abuja. But I've arranged another en-
counter first. Henry Okah is a guerrilla leader, head of the Movement for the Emancipation of the Niger Delta (MEND) and
Nigeria's most wanted man. He served more than a year in an

Angolan jail on a Nigerian arrest warrant and is now living in self-imposed exile in South Africa. A few days ago he slipped back into Lagos, and, protected by the anonymity of this limitless city, he tells me he is happy to meet at a seafood restaurant in one of the city's swankier neighborhoods. After a three-hour ride from the airport, I arrive.

Okah is more dressy than you might expect for a rebel leader: a polished bald head, a neat goatee, smart dark slacks, and a black open-necked shirt. When he talks, he has an unsettling ability to be both charming and angry. He tells me that when he started out as a militant in 2005, his discovery that a small band of men with guns cruising the creeks of southern Nigeria could hike the world price of crude oil by threatening an attack on a pipeline or kidnapping a Western oil worker initially surprised him—then encouraged him to do it again. After four years, MEND has cut Nigeria's oil output by a quarter and sometimes manages close to half. The government, finally, has promised to share the Delta's oil wealth with its people. MEND has declared a cease-fire.

But in 2009 peace negotiations are going nowhere. Okah recounts a list of false promises and examples of bad faith and official incompetence. The government even tried to buy him off, he says, offering him his own personal oil field. His clothes indicate he is not averse to money, but his patience is wearing thin. This time, he declares, he will step things up and "turn the Delta into something like Iraq." He might attack Lagos or Abuja. He chuckles: "The world has no idea how much trouble it's in." Ten months later, in September 2010, Okah is arrested in South Africa and held for extradition back to Nigeria after a multiple bomb attack in Abuja kills twelve people.

Africa has become such a byword for war and poverty that it's easy to forget it is naturally rich. It has oil (accounting for 12.65 percent of global production).[2] It has timber and farmland to spare. It has the world's largest deposits of commercial minerals and gems, producing 61 percent of the world's diamonds,[3] while South Africa alone has half the world's gold reserves. Other elements in abundance include chromium (almost all the world's reserves), bauxite (Guinea-Conakry is the world's largest producer), and enough nickel and copper, uranium and plutonium, vanadium, asbestos, cobalt, aluminum, and iron ore to make Africa a natural industrial center of the world. So what happened? How did a place so endowed with wealth manage to be so riddled with war and poverty?

Part of the answer lies in bad luck, part in bad government. Africa regularly suffers some of the world's worst natural disasters. So do Asia and the Caribbean, but Africa copes less well because it has also been ruled by some of the world's worst governments. For centuries, Africa was plundered by colonial powers. Come independence in the 1950s, 1960s, and 1970s, instead of protecting their assets, or building skills, industry, infrastructure, or general wealth—or even extracting a reasonable price for their exploitation by others—many of Africa's leaders contented themselves with having foreigners pay rent on their country's resources into Swiss bank accounts. In Nigeria's case, the World Bank estimates its generals and gangster politicians effectively stole $300 billion in this way in the three decades prior to 2006. Nigeria's own anticorruption watchdog, the Economics and Financial Crimes Commission, says they took $400 billion between 1960 and 1999—a figure that trumps not only all the aid to Nigeria over that period but all aid to Africa. It was a pattern repeated across the continent. Trampled in the elite's scramble for riches were human rights, the environment, and development. In Nigeria's oil-rich Delta, the behavior of the government and oil companies sparked MEND's civil war. It is that sorry postcolonial history that earns Africa its reputation as the "Hopeless Continent," as the *Economist* called it in 2003.

But besides bad luck and bad government, there is also bad business. Economists will tell you that, to some extent, Africa's misfortunes were inevitable. They cite an illogical-sounding phenomenon known as the "resource curse." Students of development economics like to joke that the curse describes the phenomenon of how, when a developing country discovers vast natural wealth, their professors erupt in expletives. In reality, the curse is not funny. The term was coined by British economist Richard M. Auty in 1993, when he noted that countries with rich natural resources tend to develop more slowly, more corruptly, less equitably, more violently, and with more authoritarian governments than others. One of the preeminent conundrums in economics, the curse has attracted some of its best minds. With fellow heavyweights Joseph Stiglitz and Macartan Humphreys in 2007's *Escaping the Resource Curse*, Sachs noted the "strong association between resource wealth and the likelihood of weak democratic development, corruption and civil war."

Every disaster is unique. But in Africa, the resource curse links many of its conflicts and much of its destitution. It explains the rich/poor divide in Nigeria and the rise of MEND. It accounts for the matching pattern of inequality, corruption, and instability in half a dozen other oil-producing countries around the Gulf of Guinea. It illuminates blood diamonds in Sierra Leone, Angola, Zimbabwe, and Côte d'Ivoire and how gold, tin, and cobalt fuel war in the Democratic Republic of Congo. And it helps explain the resentment felt toward miners and drillers across Africa—for the pollution they cause and the riches they take away.

The curse is often invoked by bad behavior. What should be a blessing for a poor nation turns out to be a source of ruin if it is appropriated by corrupt rulers or becomes an incentive for conflict. But Dutch Disease, a kind of resource curse subset, describes how even if governments behave themselves, their countries can still do badly. Its name derives from Holland's experience of pumping oil in the 1970s, which pushed up wages and the exchange rate, making other Dutch products more expensive to produce and export, and so raising nonoil unemployment and depressing the wider nonoil economy. Farther north, Norway managed to use oil to transform itself from an economy based on trees, fish, and ships into a sophisticated center for information technology and science. But Norway is the exception, and for Africa the lesson is clear. Business has helped to keep Africa down.

But maybe a different kind of business could lift it up. The biggest oil producer in the Niger Delta, and the biggest business in Nigeria, is ExxonMobil. With an output of around 780,000 barrels a day in 2008, its infrastructure extends to scores of rigs, lines of storage tanks, a web of pipelines, and its own airfield. In the last few years, those have all become a target for MEND.

Oil companies generally claim they don't accept the resource curse and attribute the turbulence that surrounds oil to bad government behavior. But as someone who travels the globe for ExxonMobil, often to its more remote and unstable corners, Steven Phillips is only too aware of the popular anger his company can attract. And for more than a decade, Phillips has been working on an answer. Not only for groups like MEND but something, perhaps, finally to lift the curse. The solution to one curse, he said, was to be found in fighting another: disease.

A specialist in occupational medicine, Phillips has been with the company since before it was created by combining Exxon and Mobil in 1999. In the run-up to the merger, he was part of a group that studied what the new oil giant would look like. "We had thirty refineries, forty chemical plants, and about a hundred forty thousand employees in over a hundred countries. I looked at a map of Africa and saw that ExxonMobil would be present in twenty-four African countries. Moreover, 25 percent of our upstream capital investment—in things like finding oil and gas—was going to be in Africa, at least for the next decade. And I said: 'Holy shit! Not only are we going to be huge in Africa, this is the lifeblood of our growth!'"[4]

The trouble with that, Phillips saw, was that there was plenty wrong with Africa's blood work. Tuberculosis was resurging, HIV/AIDS was "out of control," and malaria was endemic. Phillips knew taking on disease in Africa was not something an oil company would tackle out of good conscience. "Back then, it was almost taboo to mention this stuff," he says. "This was not a question of guilt or presenting the case in a moralistic way. The bottom line was we had no solid interest in it."

So Phillips decided to try "to raise the flag in a way that resonated." He conducted a company-wide survey of health hazards, making an assessment of all the risks to ExxonMobil's employees around the world: motor vehicle accidents, industrial accidents, diseases, and so on. "Two things came out on top: HIV and malaria," says Phillips. "So I presented that to the management and asked them, 'What are we going to do about this? We can't have these significant adverse impacts on our operations.'" Confronted with a case for disease control as being in their best financial interest, Phillips's bosses could only agree. For HIV, the company decided it should make free testing and treatment available. In malaria's case, Phillips argued that concentrating on the workforce alone wouldn't work. The disease was "no respecter of a fence line," he argued. "This is a war that needs a battle plan. We need to create some spending money and to start reaching out to governments where we work." Again, his bosses agreed. Harry Longwill, then ExxonMobil's director and executive vice president, asked: "Steven, how would you like a new job? We need you to make the malaria story happen for the private sector."

Phillips was attempting a remarkable change. For decades, aid and development had been the preserve of governments, charities, and individual conscience. To the question of whether they were concerned about developing the nations in which they operated, Western businesspeople would retort that business *was* development. The new breed of megaphilanthropists who emerged at the turn of the millennium took a wider view than their corporations, but that was a matter of choice rather than a matter of course. Bill Gates gave billions away. His Microsoft cofounder Paul Allen gave away $1 billion as well, but also bought two of the world's biggest yachts.[5]

The way Phillips told it, caring about malaria was also caring about the bottom line. "This was not beneficence or corporate social responsibility," he says. "We put our resources in places where they earn the best value per dollar, and this had demonstrable shareholder value. It would improve our ability to operate: if our employees and their families didn't get sick, they were going to be more productive. And it would improve our license to operate. ExxonMobil would be branded as one of the companies fighting malaria in Africa." Within months of beginning the company's malaria program, says Phillips, sick days plummeted, productivity rocketed, and ExxonMobil began to garner a name as the oil company that cared. "Chevron wasn't in malaria. BP wasn't in malaria," says Phillips. "When our CEO went to talk to African heads of states, he would say: 'Here's what we are doing in malaria. Here's what we can do for you. Here's what that investment does for education, agriculture and health.' Malaria became our differentiator. At our AGMs [annual general meetings], it became not a question of whether we should be doing it, but whether we should do more." Phillips pauses. "We had," he says, "aligned our interests with attacking malaria. Tackling malaria had become good business."

Nevertheless, "suiting up for malaria," as Phillips puts it, was virgin territory for a private company. "There was no map or precedent," he says. "I had to figure out the malaria landscape. Why was malaria in such disarray? Why were malaria programs not working? What could we do about it?" Phillips zeroed in on the poor organization of the malaria world. In particular, the Roll Back Malaria (RBM) Partnership—a coordinating body founded in 1998 to bring together governments, the UN, and aid workers—was "broken," says Phillips. It was badly run and poorly funded, its authority was unclear, and its debates were reduced to interminable squabbles between rival aid groups. Employing a standard business response, Phillips raised $3.5 million from ExxonMobil, the Gates Foundation, and others to commission the Boston Consulting Group to conduct an audit and recommend reforms. "Boston came back with a diagnosis reduced to eight actionable recommendations. So we remade RBM, and by 2006–2007 it was a well-aligned, functional global apparatus."

The remodeling of the RBM Partnership was Phillips's calling card with the aid community. "When we first started out, we got a not-so-positive reception from the NGOs or the WHO," he says. "In their view, the private sector was evil, greedy, and commercial. With the work we were doing on the RBM Partnership, the WHO declared their peace with us. We were accepted. It was a seismic shift."

Once Phillips had proved his bona fides, he set about reforming the malaria world further. Like Chambers, Phillips saw no reason to abandon business methods. On the contrary, he saw every reason why aid would benefit from some business discipline. "The private sector is accountable, by pay, by bonus, by careers—all those make people directly answerable. But the biggest issue in Africa and development is executive capacity. And one of the biggest issues in global health is that there is no reckoning of performance. People aren't measured. There are no metrics."

Phillips funded a study to discover the cost of handing out a bed net, which came back with the figure of 50 cents—far less than most NGOs were calculating and charging. Using economies of scale, he worked out a delivery program with the United States Agency for International Development (USAID) that pooled the purchase of bed nets for Nigeria, Ghana, Cameroon, and Kenya and negotiated a 50 percent bulk discount from the manufacturer. He rode around Mozambique for weeks in the cabs of Coca-Cola delivery trucks, trying to discover why they could get millions of bottles to the customer but not nets they were also given to hand out. (Answer: poor performance incentives. Coke's drivers were paid to deliver Coke, not nets.) He raised $130 million from ExxonMobil for malaria research and health programs. That included $10 million to put toward a new $100 million venture capital fund that lent money to start-ups investing in malaria, like A-Z Textile Mills in Tanzania, a bed net manufacturer partnered with the Japanese manufacturer Sumitomo, which, within five years of being established, was employing seven thousand people. In Ghana, where incomes were higher than in most of Africa, Phillips discovered some people were willing to pay for their own nets, which signaled not only the existence of a nascent commercial market—and so perhaps an eventual end to the annual problem of funding—but reassured Phillips that in Ghana a bed net would be used properly. "There was no big ideological debate," he says. "We were just trying to maximize the utility of what we were doing."

But this *was* an ideological shift. This, potentially, was how to lift the resource curse. The curse existed because neither governments nor companies cared enough about the communities in which resources were located. Both would build hospitals and schools—but more as a sop to conscience or an attempt to boost image than out of any determination to lift the population. And while it was true that only governments could fix something as big as a nation, a company that saw its fortunes tied to the well-being of the communities in which it operated was a company that would try to ensure resources benefited everyone. The traditional "exploitative" model of resource extraction in Africa, says Phillips, was "we go in, we take out, we leave problems. An attitude of: 'That's business. We pay our taxes. These other things are the province of government. It's their job.'" Exxon-Mobil was changing that model. In its areas of operation, it was working alongside African governments to deliver health care. It was spreading wealth, evening inequality, assuaging anger. It saw its profits as linked to Africa's development. Under Phillips's guidance, the world's worst disease was giving birth to a better business ethos. "Malaria is the centerpiece of a new philosophy," says Phillips. "It opens the path to a completely new way of business."

ExxonMobil was big in Nigeria. Ghana, its neighbor, didn't discover oil until 2007, and ExxonMobil was not involved. But the country had its own resource curse, one that went back centuries. And there too, malaria was the key to breaking it.

During the seventeenth and eighteenth centuries, Ghana's Ashanti tribe became one of the most advanced civilizations in Africa, with a king and an empire that took in much of West Africa. The kingdom was administered by a highly centralized bureaucracy in the Ashanti capital, Kumasi. Gold was the source of Ashanti wealth and influence—at the height of the Ashanti empire, the king was said to be able to call as many as five hundred thousand men to arms. Gold was even woven into the founding Ashanti myth. The kingdom began in 1701, it was said, when the high priest to Osei Tutu, the king of the Ashanti, called down a golden stool from the heavens.

Perhaps inevitably, gold brought trouble. The Portuguese reached Ghana as early as 1470, drawn by legends that Ghana was the location of King Solomon's Mines, and built forts along its powder-white beaches—what became known as the Gold Coast. Soon afterward, the English, the Dutch, and the Swedes also arrived and did the same. The Europeans fought among themselves and, as they vied for ascendancy, backed different sides in wars between Ghana's tribes. The nineteenth century brought a series of conflicts, with the British in particular rapaciously pursuing Ghana's natural wealth and the Ashanti defending their possessions. In a total of four wars, the British initially suffered heavy losses, then annexed the kingdom in 1896, then quickly lost their authority again when the British governor, Lord Hodgson, traveled to Kumasi and demanded to sit on the Golden Stool. Only after a three-month siege of Kumasi did Hodgson escape. The British claimed nominal rule afterward. But it was no coincidence that Ghana was the first country in Africa to win formal independence from Britain, in 1957.

Free Ghana went on to become the world's second largest exporter of gold, behind only South Africa. But the curse lingered. Foreign exploitation now came not in the form of colonialism but as Western corporate practice. Only foreign miners had the equipment to mine Ghana's gold in bulk, and many continued their operations without interruption. The new independent government took first 20 percent, then 55 percent of the shares in Ashanti Gold, which ran Ghana's main mine at Obuasi, an hour's drive south of Kumasi. But none of the revenues—neither those received by Ashanti Gold nor the government—found their way back to Obuasi. "The way gold mining was done, the perceptions of the company, it was terrible," says Steve Knowles, who joined the company in 2004. "We did a lot of damage. We took away people's land. We were polluting the ground with chemicals from the gold extraction process, including cyanide. The open pits were just left like that. The communities would say we were taking things away but giving them nothing back, and we would answer: 'But we give taxes and revenue shares to the government.' But the community didn't care about that. They wanted the money."[6]

Knowles was originally trained as an industrial hygienist. He began his career in 1970s South Africa monitoring noise, dust, and heat stress at a sugar plant in Natal (now KwaZulu Natal), South Africa. Part of his job was pest control—and in hot, humid Natal, that meant mosquitoes. In 1999, Knowles took a job working for the Australian mining giant BHP Billiton at a colossal new $1.34 billion aluminum smelter—then the world's largest—they were erecting outside Maputo in Mozambique.

The reason Knowles's experience made him a good fit for BHP Billiton and Mozambique was the Lubombo Spatial Development Initiative (LSDI). The LSDI is an opaque name for one of the best health programs in Africa. It has its foundation in an agreement signed in July 1999 by South Africa, Swaziland, and southern Mozambique. The three countries declared their mutual interest in fighting malaria in an area bounded by the Indian Ocean and the Lubombo Mountains, a range of red earth hills that rise up from the plains east of Johannesburg and run five hundred miles north through the Kruger National Park and Swaziland to beyond Maputo in southern Mozambique, the most malarious areas of all three countries. The LSDI was created out of the realization that malaria ignored borders. Good programs in South Africa and Swaziland, for example, would never succeed if mosquitoes and people were still filtering in from Mozambique. Maputo province was divided into zones. Sprayers and doctors with treatment drugs moved steadily through these, south to north.

This could have been a standard state health plan, but for one element. The LSDI agreement was specific that malaria was an economic problem. The disease was so endemic in Lubombo, the agreement read, "that no development could occur in the region if the burden of malaria was not reduced."[7] On the other hand, fixing malaria would be a boon to investment and tourism, and create jobs. As the area's biggest business, BHP Billiton stood to be the campaign's biggest beneficiary. That made it a natural host and funder for the LSDI, the more so since the company would be implementing its own malaria control program and the governments of Mozambique and South Africa were coinvestors in its plant.

The LSDI began in 2000, run by Brian Sharpe of South Africa's Medical Research Council. Knowles and BHP Billiton were Sharpe's chief implementers on the ground. Within three years, the LSDI was recording extraordinary results. Measured from the 1999–2000 malaria season, the year before the program started, malaria nose-dived. In South Africa's two border regions, KwaZulu-Natal and Mpumalanga, the incidence of malaria fell 99 percent and 86 percent by 2003–2004. In Swaziland it plummeted 90 percent. In Mozambique, parasite prevalence in children—the chosen measurement there—dropped from 60 percent to less than 10 percent. As the program continued, the results only got better. From 2000 to June 2007, in two areas of Maputo, the proportion of children who contracted malaria fell from 62 percent to 1.9 percent and from 86 percent to 12.6 percent. Meanwhile South Africa began marketing its St. Lucia wetlands wildlife park, previously the most malarious spot in the country, as "malaria free."

The LSDI worked, says Knowles, because it was run like a business. The key was marketing. He wasn't trying to sell science or technical solutions. Like any good private-sector marketer, the LSDI was selling a better life. "We don't say: 'We're spraying walls, we're killing mosquitoes,'" says Knowles. "We say: 'We're saving lives. We're creating jobs.' A malaria campaign is a tedious thing—it's the same thing over and over again. The exciting stuff is how it improves your business and your ability to live safely and comfortably."

In 2004, at the age of fifty-six, Knowles was asked by the now renamed AngloGold Ashanti[8] if he could replicate his Mozambican success at Obuasi in the green hills of central Ghana. Like ExxonMobil and BHP Billiton, says Knowles, AngloGold Ashanti "had woken up to malaria." None too soon, perhaps. As with oil, gold and malaria often overlap, and most of the twenty-two countries in which AngloGold Ashanti operated were malarious. By 2004, the company had reached the same conclusion as Phillips. "Malaria remains the most significant public health threat to AngloGold Ashanti operations in Ghana, Mali, Guinea and Tanzania," read a company statement at the time.[9]

Obuasi was a particular concern. Malaria was the biggest and most lethal disease in the town, accounting for 48 percent of illness and 22 percent of deaths at the mine hospital. That was blowing a big hole in the bottom line. The company calculated its hospital was seeing 6,800 malaria patients a month in 2005, 2,500 of whom were mine employees (out of a total workforce of 8,000). Even if each sick worker only took three days off, that was 7,500 shifts a month lost to malaria. To make up the shortfall, the company was employing 1,600 more workers than it needed. Treating sick workers was also costing it $55,000 a month.

For Knowles, the chance to create a malaria program from scratch, and with a generous budget, was an opportunity to combine "all the best ideas and procedures from all the programs I had worked on." As in Mozambique, Knowles reckoned malaria was a business problem and should be tackled as one. For too long, he says, malaria programs had been the preserve of scientists and academics, experts at investigating ways of stopping malaria in a lab but amateurs at applying their ideas on the ground. But it was precisely their dexterity in tough environments that had made companies such as ExxonMobil and Anglo-Gold Ashanti the world leaders they were. "The aid guys, the UN guys, the academics, they sit in Geneva with twenty centimeters of snow outside and say: 'If everyone uses a net, there will be no more malaria.' Well, that's true, but in reality people don't go to bed from 6 PM and rise at 6 AM. It always takes a human element. To run a malaria control program in the developing world is the same as running a successful company there. It takes people like me. It takes implementers."

At Obuasi, Knowles decided, implementation would be total. To cover Obuasi's population of two hundred thousand, Anglo-Gold Ashanti would train 116 workers to spread out across the town and the surrounding area. They would spray each of the 139,000 buildings, including 36,000 houses, every five months. They would put up nets on every bed and screens on every window, and distribute repellents to every home. They would treat every piece of stagnant water with larvicide. And they would make malaria treatment drugs available to everyone. Knowles projected the cost, including wages, sixty spray pumps, eight trucks, and nine trailers, at $1.7 million a year in 2005 and $1.3 million thereafter. To save money, he offered to run the program from a disused mine building.

The results were just as spectacular as Mozambique. Cases of malaria treated at the mine hospital fell from 6,800 a month in 2005 to 2,800 by the end of 2006 and 1,000 by the end of 2007. In the surrounding area, they fell from more than 10,000 a month to 5,000. The proportion of the workforce contracting the disease every month decreased from just under 25 percent to 4 percent. The cost to the company of treating malaria plunged from $55,000 a month in 2005 to $8,235 in 2010—itself a saving of $560,000 a year. Days off sick because of malaria plummeted from 6,983 a month to just 282, meaning the company could save another $5 million a year that it had been paying for extra labor to cover the gaps.

Phillips had made the business case for malaria. Now Knowles had—twice—proved it. On March 12, 2007, Knowles presented his results to a private sector forum on malaria sponsored by the

Global Business Coalition at the Brookings Institution, the renowned Washington think tank. In attendance were Chambers and Phillips, now an advisor to Chambers. "The results were astounding," says Chambers. "And I remember Steve Knowles made this clear: this was about the economic interests of Anglo-Gold Ashanti. It was in their interests to protect people. They could not tolerate so many absences due to malaria. You could see people file that away. 'We shouldn't have to be pushed to do this. We shouldn't do it out of altruism. This should be part of our business plan.'"[10]

AngloGold Ashanti's transformation from Ghanaian asset stripper to a partner in Ghana's development was made official shortly afterward when it was appointed coordinator of the country's national malaria program. For the Ghanaian government, appointing a private-sector company made sense. It increasingly saw malaria in financial terms. "The total cost to our economy from malaria in 2007 was $760 million," said the then Ghanaian health minister, George Sipa Adja Yankey. "That's 10 percent of our GDP." The new job was also a logical extension of the work Knowles was already doing at Obuasi, where the data strongly suggested the program needed to grow. Knowles suffered his worst reversal in November 2006, when two thousand of Obuasi's mine workers traveled to Kumasi for the funeral of a local chief. Outside Knowles's operating area for the first time in months, eight hundred people had contracted malaria.

With government support, AngloGold Ashanti applied to the Global Fund for a grant of $133 million, proposing to scale up the Obuasi model to the forty most malarious districts in Ghana, about a quarter of the country. The Global Fund agreed. In early 2009 AngloGold Ashanti became the first private company ever to be approved for a Global Fund grant. The transformation was complete. Business had become aid, and a national aid program was now run by a business. "Yeah, sure, a few people ask me: 'Why are you doing this?'" says Knowles. "'It's not your bloody job. It's the government's job.' But more and more people understand that what's happening here is a fundamental shift." Combining business and aid worked, says Knowles, because it worked for everyone. Ghana got to control malaria. AngloGold Ashanti got to cut its costs. And a small corner of Africa got to banish the resource curse. "After all those years when nobody liked us," says Knowles, "now people love us. The hospitals are empty. The children aren't getting sick seven or eight times a year. The housewives get a free pest control service. Obuasi has changed beyond recognition. It's a great, prosperous, happy little town."

CHAPTER 6

Levers of Power

As business began to see the value in fighting malaria, so the disease also moved up government agendas. The shift began in 1993, when the World Bank's annual World Development Report made the link between disease and economics when it quantified, for the first time, the relative burdens that different diseases placed on efforts by the poor world to develop. Malaria and tuberculosis emerged as far bigger constraints than other diseases. Christian Lengeler at the Swiss Tropical Institute says with that discovery, "the world was changed forever. For the first time, we had hard evidence of how important these diseases were, not just to health, but to prosperity and development."[1]

Still, it wasn't until October 1997 that the World Bank, various UN agencies, and donor governments such as the US and Britain met in Washington to discuss how, after three decades of dormancy, they might revive efforts to fight malaria. Economists like Jeffrey Sachs and celebrity campaigners such as Bono and Bob Geldof were noisily demanding action on health in the poor world, and the world was gradually responding. The meeting decided to form the Roll Back Malaria Partnership to coordinate the international battle against the disease.

Back then, few people had any idea of what that fight might look like. Lengeler did. The last bed net trial had finally wrapped in 1996, and Lengeler was asked to present the data in Washington. The results showed how powerful a tool the simple bed net could be. They also demonstrated the bigger the campaign, the better. And bigger, of course, meant money. In 1996, the WHO spent $9 million on malaria control and prevention in Africa. Even in 1999, the total funding for malaria around the world was just $33 million. After he presented his results, says Lengeler, the consensus at the meeting was "'this is very convincing, this is what we need to do' and an eventual $700 million was raised to fund the fight against malaria."

That first surge in funding was the foundation of what would later grow into a second global campaign against malaria. It had many elements. In 1999, the Millennium Development Goals made tackling malaria a priority. On April 25, 2000, at a meeting in Abuja, Nigeria, forty-four African countries, including nineteen heads of state, committed themselves to halving malaria deaths by 2010. Meanwhile, new malaria-specific charities, campaign groups, and fund-raising organizations sprang up with names like the Malaria Consortium, Against Malaria, Nothing But Nets, and Africa Fighting Malaria. Established aid groups began reviving or expanding their malaria programs.

Malariology was also staging a comeback. Bill and Melinda Gates set up the Bill & Melinda Gates Foundation in 1999, and by 2002–2003 they were giving out hundreds of millions of dollars a year to fund health projects in the poor world, with

HIV/AIDS and malaria identified as priorities. Early on they invested in the development of new malaria drugs, cures, and preventions, setting up the Malaria Vaccine Initiative (MVI) to hasten work on discovering the secret of malaria immunity; the Medicines for Malaria Venture (MMV) to produce new antimalarial prophylactics and treatment drugs; and the Foundation for Innovative New Diagnostics (FIND) to develop more accurate and rapid testing for malaria and other diseases. Funding was suddenly available for studies into drugs, insecticides, vaccines, even fantastical-sounding ideas such as a microchip to diagnose malaria,[2] irradiating male mosquitoes to sterilize them,[3] and interfering with mosquito sex lives.[4] Brian Greenwood, who had left Africa after more than three decades for a position at the London School of Hygiene and Tropical Medicine, found himself on the receiving end. "Shortly after I arrived in 2000–2001, we got a grant from the Gates Foundation for $40 million," says Greenwood. "And that was just the first. The next one was nearly $60 million. I thought I had one more job in me. I just hadn't realized it was going to be quite such a big job."[5]

Bill and Melinda Gates also drew pharmaceutical giants into the campaign. The heart of any drug company is its research and development laboratory, where new drugs are discovered and refined. But science is expensive, and since malaria is a poor-world disease, no company could justify spending hundreds of millions of dollars on developing drugs to prevent or treat malaria if it could not recoup the cost. That was something the world's richest man could help with. Through funds like MVI and MMV, scientists at universities and research institutes were paid to develop new drugs or treatments. Once a breakthrough was discovered, the innovations were then passed to drug companies for refining and manufacturing into final products for which, since agencies like the World Bank and the Global Fund were now subsidizing them, there now was a viable market.

This wasn't only about money for the drug companies. But as with ExxonMobil and AngloGold Ashanti, it was always about self-interest. The image and commercial prospects of big pharmaceutical companies in Africa had been damaged by two controversies at the turn of the millennium: less than ethical drugs trials in West Africa and the industry's fight to prevent Africans from buying anyone's HIV/AIDS drugs but their own. Tadataka "Tachi" Yamada, head of Global Health at the Gates Foundation, says he quit as head of research and development at GlaxoSmithKline when the pharmaceutical industry launched a legal case to prevent South Africa from using generic HIV/AIDS drugs. (The drug giants lost.) This was more than public relations could fix. Drug companies needed to remake their entire way of business. Occasionally manufacturing medicine for reasons other than profit was one way to do that. By the end of the decade, Merck was supplying Botswana's entire national HIV/AIDS program with drugs for free and had given a potential new malaria treatment drug to MMV for no charge. GlaxoSmithKline was developing another malaria vaccine, which it was pledging not to patent but to share.

And still the campaign grew. In 2002, the Global Fund to Fight AIDS, Tuberculosis and Malaria was formed as a pooling body to act as a single collector and distributor of hundreds of millions, then billions, of dollars in Western government donations for the three diseases. In April 2005, the World Bank inaugurated a malaria program for the first phase of which—campaigns in twenty countries over three years—it set aside $500 million. Then that June, President George W. Bush announced the formation of the President's Malaria Initiative (PMI).

The story of how Bush came to plow billions into fighting malaria illustrates how the malaria campaign was founded as much on self-interest—even political expediency—as good intentions. By 2005, despite winning reelection, the Bush White House was painfully aware that history would judge it poorly. Iraq was a disaster, Afghanistan was another quagmire, and the scandals were mounting—Guantanamo Bay, Abu Ghraib, Fallujah, the rendition of terror suspects to foreign torture chambers—while the terrorist threat remained undiminished, as attacks in Bali, Madrid, and London showed. That same year Hurricane Katrina washed away what little credibility the administration had left.

Through it all, British prime minister Tony Blair had been a loyal ally. Blair's stance was costing him heavily in Britain, where the war in Iraq was unpopular. Bush knew he owed Blair. He also knew Africa was a pet project for Blair and his finance minister, Chancellor of the Exchequer Gordon Brown. As early as October 2001, Blair had told delegates of the annual conference of his Labour Party that African poverty was a "scar on our consciences" that would "become deeper and angrier" if not healed.

In the run-up to a G8 summit in Gleneagles, Scotland, in June 2005, Blair declared he was going use his position as host to ensure the development of Africa headed the agenda. "Tony Blair was taking a major interest in putting Africa on the map at Gleneagles," says a US medical expert with access to the White House at the time. "Britain was hosting the summit, and would run the show, and Blair was all about ramping up pledges for Africa." At a previous summit, the G8 committed its members to making foreign aid 0.7 percent of GDP. But come early 2005, US contributions were just 0.17 percent, and in May, with the G8 just weeks away, Blair announced he would be visiting Washington. "The word was Blair was going to shake down Bush," says the expert. "So Bush said: 'We have to get ready for this. We are going to respond to Tony. He's our friend, and we want to keep him as a friend. So what's our response?'"[6]

Bush's team said the US could not commit to raising its donations to 0.7 percent of GDP overnight. Such an increase would involve massive tax increases, the kind of raises against which Bush had campaigned in two successful elections. But, the White House staffers agreed, they needed to give Blair something. "They interviewed a whole bunch of experts in the public health sector," says one of those who was called in, "and we told them: 'In terms of a disease that is preventable and curable, it's malaria. It's doable. It does not have the political complications of HIV. Plus, this is already a rallying point for donors. The private sector is stepping up. The Gates Foundation is stepping up. This is a winner.'"[7]

The idea of a presidential push against a developing world disease had precedent. In 2003, Bush had set up the $15 billion, five-year President's Emergency Plan for AIDS Relief (PEPFAR) to fund prevention programs and treatment drugs in Africa.[8] Bush also agreed with Colin Powell that the roots of rage derived from inequality. Though his administration's foreign policy is chiefly remembered for Bush's tough-talking vows of vengeance after 9/11, and the subsequent invasions of Afghanistan and Iraq, military might was just one way Bush was trying to counter those who felt the US was an overbearing, overaffluent presence in the world. In Africa—no less suspicious of the US and viewed by the Pentagon as a rising security threat—Bush preferred giving to guns. By 2005, he had tripled overseas aid to the continent. When Blair arrived in Washington in May that year, Bush said he was going to double aid again—and this time, the focus would be malaria. As an initial step in what would become known as the President's Malaria Initiative, Bush announced the US would spend $1.2 billion fighting malaria over the next five years by providing Tanzania, Uganda, and Angola with insecticide-treated bed nets, treatment drugs, and insecticide spraying.

Initially Bush concentrated on the how. As he left for Gleneagles in June, Bush said he was aware of the growing criticism of aid, and agreed with much of it. The pitfalls of creating "passive recipients of money" were evident. "Overcoming extreme poverty requires partnership, not paternalism. Economic development is not something we do for countries, it is something they achieve with us. . . . Without economic and social freedom, without the rule of law and effective, honest government, international aid has little impact or value. Economic aid that expects little will achieve little. Economic aid that expects much can help to change the world."[9] Malaria, said the president, would be the arena in which the US would try a new type of aid. This time assistance would mean just that: available only to African governments who would, and could, run the show themselves.

Where the US president leads, others follow. Britain immediately announced another £200 million for malaria. German chancellor Angela Merkel formed the European Alliance Against Malaria (EAAM), a group of ten organizations to campaign and coordinate. "We went from a few million to billions," said Lengeler. "It was huge."

It was huge. But still it wasn't enough. Sachs calculated the need for Africa alone at $3 billion a year. The new resources, unimaginable a few years before, were insufficient to cover that single continent for a single year, let alone the entire world for several years. Nor was everyone on board. Doubters included the then secretary-general of the WHO, South Korean Lee Jong-wook who, mindful of the failure of the WHO's previous campaign, told a 2004 meeting of the Roll Back Malaria Partnership at the WHO's headquarters in Geneva, according to one US health professional present: "Malaria is not a winnable war. This will be the world's Vietnam, and the WHO will not get involved in any significant way."[10]

After his January 2006 trip to Kenya, Chambers had cofounded his own malaria NGO, Malaria No More, with News Corporation's then president, Peter Chernin. To Chambers and Chernin, the way to ramp up the campaign yet further was obvious: leverage. Moreover, two of the three elements of a Newark plan were already in place—political leadership and investment, whether it came from aid agencies or business—and as head of one of the world's largest media companies, Chernin said he could bring the third. It was Chambers's job to fit all three together.

But before the malaria world could perform in a triangle of leverage, it had to function by itself. And as Steven Phillips had already discovered, it did not do that well. Malaria lacked coordination. Despite the reforms Phillips had helped implement at Roll Back Malaria, the confusion had only worsened with the rising interest in the disease: the malaria world now comprised a bewildering sea of acronyms—WHO, RBM, PMI, EAAM, MMV—with equally mixed-up responsibilities. Suprotik Basu, then working for the World Bank as a health specialist, remembers how Chambers used his new NGO to convene "a meeting of a bunch of players in the malaria world to understand where the gaps were. The more he dug into the malaria space, the more he realized part of the problem was that malaria was really fragmented."[11] Says Chambers, "It had become clear that we needed everyone to come together under one umbrella."[12]

Chambers went back to the Newark plan: start with the politics. The single most influential political office on earth was being brought to bear in the fight against malaria, and Chambers wasn't going to waste it. Chernin and Chambers arranged a meeting with Michael Gerson, Bush's speechwriter, and Gary Edson, whose influence inside the White House was described by his many titles: deputy national security advisor, deputy assistant for international economic affairs, deputy national economic advisor, and chief US negotiator at the G8 summits, as well as founder of PEPFAR.

Chambers told the pair: "This is a wonderful opportunity to show the positive side of President Bush. Forty percent of the children dying in Africa from malaria are Muslim. Imagine if we could get together a united global effort to stop that."

Gerson and Edson approved. They set up a meeting with Bush's closest advisor, Karen Hughes, and again Chambers made his pitch.

"Could we have a White House conference on malaria?" asked Hughes.

"Could we make it a summit?" asked Chambers.

"Let's make it a summit," replied Hughes.

On December 14, 2006, in the fog and early snow of a Washington winter, Bush convened a White House summit on malaria. Held behind the grand colonnades of the National Geographic Society building, six blocks north of the White House, the list of seven hundred participants read—as it was—like a guest list at an unlikely arranged marriage. Representing aid and development was the then World Bank chief Paul Wolfowitz; Melinda Gates of the Bill & Melinda Gates Foundation; Ann Veneman, head of UNICEF; Richard Feachem, then executive director of the Global Fund; and the new Hong Kong–born director-general of the World Health Organization, Margaret Chan. On the other side of the aisle was the corporate West: managers from Exxon-Mobil, Marathon Oil, and Anglo American and a host of Wall Street, media, and Silicon Valley tycoons. Chaperones for this meeting of worlds were Bush, his wife, Laura, and Secretary of State Condoleezza Rice.

The matchmaking seemed to work. Aid and business flirted warmly with each other. Global Fund founder Richard Feachem singled out the LSDI in Mozambique for particular praise, calling it "Africa's most successful malaria control program today." The WHO's Margaret Chan drew applause from businessmen in the room when she said: "As a United Nations agency, oftentimes we are criticized for being very bureaucratic, for being very insular. We need to take inspiration from [the corporate sector]. If a soft drink can get to the farthest corner of the world, why can't our drugs and bed nets?"[13]

Steven Phillips repaid the compliment by making the reverse case: why aid was good for business. ExxonMobil had become involved in fighting malaria six years before, he said, because as a business it couldn't afford not to. "When you look at a map of Africa and overlay the pattern of malaria intensity with oil operations, there is a striking confluence. It is a strange coincidence that where there is oil, there are mosquitoes. ExxonMobil is here today because our business presence in Africa caused us to witness firsthand the devastating health and economic impact malaria has had on our workforce."

ExxonMobil had spent $30 million in six years and sixteen countries on advocacy, research, nets, drugs, and evaluation. In that time, just one ExxonMobil employee had contracted the disease. Phillips said he believed that showed malaria could be beaten and that business had much to offer the effort. Underlining why coordination was so important with malaria, he added that from working alongside African governments, the UN, and other aid groups as a partner in Africa's development, Exxon-Mobil had discovered the best results were achieved when everyone worked together. "No one sector, government, or institution can solve the problem alone," said Phillips. "But when we reach a similar position regarding a business opportunity, we share the risks and rewards by forming a joint venture. And what does that take? Organization. This parasite thrives on disorganized human systems. Conversely, it is defeated by collaboration."

As Chambers hoped, the summit also offered the promise of more money. The World Bank's Wolfowitz admitted: "In the first half of this decade none of us were putting sufficient priority on malaria." Noting that was now being partially corrected by fresh funding from his organization, Wolfowitz added: "There is more coming." The Global Fund's Feachem also said his organization was ready to hand out billions more.

Bush spoke last. That a million Africans should die of malaria every year was unacceptable, he said. The US eliminated malaria nearly sixty years earlier. The disparity was intolerable. "We know exactly what it takes to prevent and treat the disease," he said. "The only question is whether we have the will to act."

For the first time, Bush also set out why malaria in Africa was a US priority. The president declared he had no choice. The US, and big business in particular, had a moral duty to offset the global inequality that their existence represented. Three times Bush repeated the phrase "To whom much is given, much is required." Business also had much more to offer besides money, said Bush. The Gates Foundation was a "fantastic example of social entrepreneurship. It was caused to be because of fantastic business entrepreneurship. It is now using the business acumen, and the rewards of being smart, to fund unbelievable programs."

And then in words that might have been written by Chambers, Bush added that if malaria weighed on the conscience of some, and prompted them to act, that was good. But fighting malaria was in the self-interest of all. "We're sending a broader message about America's purpose in the world. In this new century there is a great divide, between those who place no value on human life and rejoice in the suffering of others, and those who believe that every life has matchless value, and answer suffering with compassion and kindness. The contrast is vivid, and the position of America is clear. We will lead the cause of freedom, justice, and hope. . . . We also know that nations with free, healthy, prosperous people will be sources of stability, not breeding grounds for extremists and hate and terror." Business had to understand that "it's in your corporate interests that the people of Africa see that you're willing to invest in the future of their countries." The same applied to every US citizen. "By helping others the American people must understand we help ourselves. By making the world more hopeful, we make the world more peaceful."

Chambers had pulled off the all-time piece of leverage. He had brought the biggest name in world politics together with the world's biggest donors and corporations in front of the world's media. It was the ultimate Newark triangle.

Notwithstanding the achievement, Chambers was disheartened. For leverage to succeed, the different elements have to work together. But inside the malaria world, the big players barely seemed to know each other, let alone be able to function in unison. Off camera, Chambers chaired a side meeting with the heads of the malaria NGOs and funders. One attendee mentioned her organization had made a large grant to help fight malaria in Nigeria; as far as she knew, no one else was aware of it. Feachem noted the poor quality of applications to the Global Fund from African governments, which meant only 20 percent were succeeding. Chambers exploded. "If all of you were in the for-profit world," he intoned, "you'd be bankrupt. You can't go on like this. You've got to get it together."

For the next few months, Chambers busied himself with Malaria No More. "Just meeting with partners and friends and creating the conversation to see what it would take to get more money," he says. "Just building and building, much like you would do with a business." He met leaders of a Lutheran denomination in the US that maintained a wide missionary network on the continent and had also decided to raise funds for malaria. He helped bring a roll call of businesses with big Africa operations—Bayer, BHP Billiton, Chevron, De Beers, DHL, GlaxoSmithKline, Heineken, Marathon Oil, the consultants McKinsey, Newmont Mining, Novartis, Pfizer, Royal Dutch Shell, Standard Chartered Bank, and Sumitomo—to Knowles's March 2007 lecture at Brookings.

He also flew back to Africa as part of an effort to visit each of the most malarious countries and "see what their plans were and how they could be helped." He handed out bed nets in Uganda. He visited "a few clinics where children were dying of malaria." He found his resolve hardening. "The worst thing is you see their eyes open. All you see is white. And you know they're not coming back. You see their teenage mother sitting there, and you can see that they do not have any hope. Put that together with the notion of a $10 net, and I don't know how anyone could resist wanting to solve this problem. Especially someone like me, with the experience in taking on problems and with the resources to do it." Speed was becoming ever more important to Chambers. "Every minute you delay, you are losing children. Somebody goes on vacation and does not have their phone on? That's unacceptable. Bureaucratic delays? That's unacceptable. Any pause is unacceptable."

In Rwanda, Chambers met President Kagame and visited the museum in Kigali commemorating the 1994 genocide. There, surveying the glass boxes of skulls that make up the remains of some two hundred fifty thousand people, Chambers had another epiphany. "It occurred to me that malaria was a genocide. How was it that we had a disease that killed a million-plus people a year, and we let it happen? This was a genocide of apathy."

The opposite of apathy was involvement. Chambers set about using Malaria No More to draw in everyone he could. A glance at the organization's board confirms it is a charity with a difference. The usual suspects are there. Representing aid are senior figures from UNICEF, the Gates Foundation, the Red Cross, Care, and the UN Foundation. Representing science are Richard Feachem and Brian Greenwood, among others. That was where most aid groups would have stopped. But Chambers also reached out to religion, where he found Rick Warren, the leading evangelical pastor in the US. From the sports world, he took the chair of the Special Olympics, Timothy Shriver, and, later, the soccer player David Beckham and the British tennis player Andy Murray. From entertainment, he recruited the Senegalese singer Youssou N'Dour to become a board member, while Ashton Kutcher, Demi Moore, Bono, and P. Diddy lent support. From Africa, he drew in heads of state from across the continent as informal consultants. And from business, he took in a swath of leaders, including the CEO of LinkedIn, the cofounder of Priceline.com, and an executive vice president of Time Warner. To Chambers and Chernin, the last group—business—was key. "Malaria is not a science problem," says Chernin. "It's a logistics problem, a business problem. There's an opportunity here for business to provide the urgency and focus on results, organization, and logistics, the kind of thing business is good at."

If Chambers's approach was unusual, so was his manner, recalls Gabrielle Fitzgerald, senior program director at the Gates Foundation. "It was around September 2006 that this man I had never heard of called Ray Chambers began showing up at all these malaria meetings," she says. "He had founded this thing called Malaria No More, and he was like a bull in a china shop. He wanted to do something on malaria, but he didn't know what. And the malaria world is small. To have this guy come in and mix things up, everyone was asking, 'Who is this guy?' It was kind of a rough start. Then he got the White House to host the malaria summit, and Malaria No More and Chambers kind of found their sea legs."[14]

But Chambers was still doing things his own way. One problem with marketing the malaria cause, he decided, was that it lacked a good slogan. Like many others, Chambers had been impressed by an April 2006 *Sports Illustrated* column by Rick Reilly in which Reilly, by connecting sports nets with malaria nets, made the case for malaria. "If you have ever gotten a thrill by throwing, kicking, knocking, dunking, slamming, putting up, cutting down or jumping over a net, please go to a special site we've set up through the United Nations Foundation. . . . Sports is nothing but net. So next time you think of a net, go to that website and click yourself happy. Ten bucks means a kid might get to live. Make it $20 and more kids are saved." Chambers began repeating a simplified version of Reilly's message—"$10 buys a net, saves a child's life"—like a mantra.

The UN Foundation, which had originally come up with the $10-a-bed-net campaign, took Reilly's premise to the National Basketball Association and US Major League soccer authorities and, with funding from the Gates Foundation, created the Nothing But Nets campaign. The effect of streamlining the message was "massive," says Fitzgerald. "It moved people, and it began seeping into pop culture." American football players began backing the malaria campaign. Rock stars talked about it. So did actors. One eight-year-old girl from Pennsylvania, Katherine Commale, raised $100,000 for Nothing But Nets in three years.

The idea of linking malaria to something fun like sports appealed to Chambers. He had little time for traditional aid-group publicity drives. For decades, aid and development charities have followed a set format for, as industry jargon has it, "raising awareness": an image of a destitute African child in some kind of distress, preferably in black and white, perhaps taken by an eminent war photographer, overlaid with a message demanding the reader forgo a trivial amount of money and save a baby. It was not an approach Chambers liked. It was depressing, and depression was niche. Far more engaging, he thought, was a cause presented as something people might like to join rather than something they ought. It should be enjoyable. And Chernin was in a position to help: News Corporation owned Fox, which happened to broadcast the biggest entertainment show on US television, the talent show *American Idol*. And so on April 24, 2007, Fox broadcast a special edition "Idol Gives Back."

The show was put together by two Britons, *Idol* producer Simon Fuller and Richard Curtis, director of *Four Weddings and a Funeral*, *Notting Hill*, and *Love Actually* and producer of the biennial British telethon *Comic Relief*. Like Chambers, Curtis was tired of presenting Africa as a place of continuous calamity. "I've worked for twenty years on TV programs that fund-raise for Africa," he says, "and always, because we're trying to move people into giving money, we've had to concentrate on some of the harshest things." That image making had worked too well, said Curtis. People thought Africa was hopeless, and that was both unhelpful and inaccurate. "I once read a statistic that people in Africa, when asked if they are happy, are more likely to answer yes than people in Europe or the US. I also believe that if people can really believe in the rich, normal life of people in Africa, we won't be happy to have millions die there."[15] Fuller was also pleased to come on board. As a boy, he had direct experience of malaria. "My father contracted malaria during his time as a pilot in Burma during the Second World War and would often talk of its consequences," he says. "And I lived in Ghana for five years as a child, and malaria and its consequences were an everyday reality for me. So I understood the importance of prevention and medical care needed to combat malaria at a very early age."[16]

Malaria was a serious subject, and "Idol Gives Back" had serious moments. Presenters Ryan Seacrest and Simon Cowell recorded short sequences of themselves traveling in Africa and sleeping under a net in a village. But its main attraction was a show-business lineup that was all but unprecedented. Fronting the two-hour special with Seacrest was Ellen DeGeneres. Stars who appeared included actors Kevin Bacon, Antonio Banderas, Helena Bonham Carter, Tom Cruise, Matt Damon, Hugh Grant, Goldie Hawn, Keira Knightley, Hugh Laurie, Rob Lowe, Ewan McGregor, Helen Mirren, Gwyneth Paltrow, Miss Piggy, and the Simpsons. Musicians included the Black Eyed Peas, Bono, Michael Bublé, Annie Lennox, and Madonna. Celine Dion performed a duet with a hologram of Elvis Presley.

Among the 26.4 million Americans who tuned in, ensuring "Idol Gives Back" topped the ratings, were hundreds of bloggers. Their breathless reviews provide an illuminating snapshot of how Curtis and Fuller managed to make compulsive entertainment out of a deadly disease. On a website called Wild Bluff Media, "Matt" wrote:

> Ben Stiller comes on and does some good jokes about all the movies he's been in. Next he lets us know that he plans to sing non-stop until the show has raised $200 billion. He's actually going to sing the very same song the entire time. Please, donate now to help stop Ben. Ryan and Simon return in their video to the children and families they visited on their trip to Africa. One of the young children they visit is a 12-year-old boy who lost both parents and is now the leader of his family. It's a very sad story and is really motivating to support the cause. Our first results reveal for the night is with Melinda Doolittle and . . . she is safe. No kidding. Of course she is, she's great! Paula's video gives us a tour of a Boys & Girls Club. Il Divo is the next group up. Guess who founded this group?? That's right, Simon Cowell did! Sheesh. Shameless plugging of your own stuff during a charity event. The important message from this part though is that every 3 seconds a child dies in extreme poverty. Alright, Jack Black is on stage! Awesome! Another video highlights the rapid death rate in Africa. So many children are dying from malaria every day. A packet of medicine costing only $2 can save the lives of four children. One such child that our camera crew comes across and drives to the hospital is not so fortunate and dies before they can get there. 50 cents worth of medicine would have saved that baby. It's a crushing situation to see. Kelly Clarkson is up next and gives an amazing performance.[17]

The money poured in. News Corporation pledged to donate 10 cents for every vote made to the show for the first fifty million calls—up to $5 million—while its MySpace arm created a special profile page for the event. Donations from viewers were accepted by phone and online, and by May 1 the final total collected was more than $75 million. More important to Chambers than the money was how *American Idol* leveraged a new profile for malaria. "Before Idol, only 20 percent of the US saw malaria as a current health crisis," he said. "That went up to over 50 percent."

The goal of the new campaign was initially open-ended: save lives. On October 17, 2007, Bill and Melinda Gates gathered three hundred scientists and funders together in Seattle with the intention of refining that. There had already been rumblings among malariologists and epidemiologists about what their well-meaning and well-funded but, in the view of many, underqualified leaders were going to ask of them. More than a few cynics were openly mocking Chambers's choice of name for his organization, while Melinda Gates's comments at the White House summit—that "wiping out malaria could join the eradication of smallpox as one of the greatest achievements in human history"—had been studiously ignored.

Bill and Melinda Gates were determined that would not happen again. "Advances in science and medicine, promising research, and the rising concern of people around the world represent an historic opportunity not just to treat malaria or to control it—but to chart a long-term course to eradicate it," Melinda Gates told the scientists. Lest anyone was in any doubt, Bill underscored the new ambition: "We will not stop working until malaria is eradicated."[18] For a second time, the world would be taking on malaria. This time, the aim was to wipe it off the planet forever.

CHAPTER 7

Global Network

Bill and Melinda Gates had set the goal of eradicating the disease. But who was going to lead the fight? Chambers suggested to WHO director-general Margaret Chan that she put herself forward. Chan disagreed. She had all the world's diseases on her plate—HIV/AIDS, tuberculosis, swine flu, avian flu, SARS, dengue, cholera, river blindness, and Ebola, as well as malaria. She couldn't concentrate on just one, and that's what malaria needed. "You should be the first UN special envoy for Malaria," she told Chambers. She made the same suggestion to UN secretary-general Ban Ki-Moon. "You could see Ray was the guy to get this done," she says.[1]

Chambers was unsure about taking a job at the UN. "I just wanted to keep working on what I was doing," he says.[2] Basu, who had left the World Bank to join Malaria No More as its managing director in October 2007, remembers discussing the issue with Chambers. "The two of us debated. Ray doesn't like press or giving speeches, and he really didn't want to be bound by the rules and regulations of the UN. On the plus side, he was trying to achieve such a wholesale change in the way that you approach aid that there was no way he could do it as chair of a small NGO in the US, no matter how rich he was."[3]

Chambers decided the title of special envoy would give him and malaria the standing—and the leverage—both needed. Ban Ki-Moon was enthused about the possibilities a businesslike approach might offer. A meeting was scheduled between the two at the UN building in New York. "It was a good discussion, and Ray accepted," says Basu, "and then as a last order of business they asked Ray to agree to the terms of reference for the job, and handed him a five-page document that said: 'Ray Chambers will do X, Y, and Z, the WHO will do X, Y, and Z to help Ray Chambers. We will have this many meetings with the WHO to agree on which countries we would target, the WHO/UN will agree to finance four trips a year, business class for the special envoy, etc., etc., etc.' And Ray said: 'What the hell is this? This doesn't exist in my world.' He told me: 'It's your job to get rid of all this. All I want is something that says: *Ray Chambers will do everything in his power to end malaria.*'" Basu laughs. "So I call the secretary-general's office and tell them this is a special envoy not like other special envoys. And we negotiate the terms down to Ray Chambers doing his utmost to end deaths from malaria and the UN supporting him with a salary of $1 a year. It was worlds colliding."

In February 2008, Ban Ki-Moon announced Chambers's appointment as the first UN special envoy for malaria. One of the biggest and most ambitious campaigns ever undertaken by the aid world would be led by a Wall Street millionaire whose background and methods made him, at first glance, anathema to almost everyone in that world. On April 9, a second "Idol Gives

Back" with a similarly star-studded cast—this time also including presidential candidate Hillary Clinton and Blair's successor as British prime minister, Gordon Brown—raised another $64 million.[4] And if anyone doubted a sea change was under way, on April 25, World Malaria Day, at the UN Building in New York, Ban Ki-Moon announced that not only was eradication of malaria the goal but as a first step his new special envoy would oversee the global distribution of a bed net to everyone in the world who needed one by the end of 2010, a timeframe of a little more than two and a half years. This was a "bold but achievable" vision, said Ban. The burden of the disease was "unacceptable—all the more so because malaria is preventable and treatable." Writing in the *Guardian* newspaper, he added: "We have the resources and the know-how. But we have less than 1,000 days before the end of 2010. So let's get to work."[5]

Chambers recognized he had just been set one of the most intimidating aid targets ever attempted. "People said: 'This is just another one of those goals that people put out and which they have no chance of meeting,'" he said. It wasn't only the number of bed nets that was daunting. Chambers was going to be cajoling Western donors to part with billions, persuading African presidents that this was in their interest, convincing prickly aid workers to surrender themselves to his plan when most of them considered it unworkable—and him untouchable on principle—and then pushing them hard to implement it. He would be trying to coordinate a motley crew of independent partners: the Global Fund, the President's Malaria Initiative, the Gates Foundation, the WHO, UNICEF, Britain's Department for International Development (DfID), and UNITAID, a UN agency specializing in innovative aid finance. And he would be attempting all this without formally controlling any of the money or the people it would take to do it. If he were to have any hope of success, Chambers would need some unusual skills in the people around him.

Chambers already had Suprotik Basu, known to his colleagues as "Protik." A thirty-two-year-old graduate in health economics from Johns Hopkins University, Basu had been a health and development specialist at the World Bank for six years. After Wolfowitz became Bank president in March 2005, the former US deputy secretary of defense had made alleviation of poverty in Africa a priority and malaria a focus of that effort. Basu was part of a malaria team that reported directly to Wolfowitz every quarter. He found Wolfowitz and his ability to focus a large organization like the Bank on a single issue impressive. "He was one of the more intimidating and bright guys I have ever worked with," says Basu. "And when I met Ray in New York as he was getting involved in malaria, there was a lot that I applied to him from Paul, about what can happen when you have a really strong leader with skin in the game." In October 2007, Basu asked his World Bank bosses for two years' leave. "I just told them: 'I really want to do this. I really think we could do something.'" His bosses were more than supportive. Three years later, Basu would muse: "I'm actually still technically on leave from the Bank."

In 2008, Chambers moved thirty-seven blocks north from the offices of Malaria No More to the new UN special envoy's office, in reality Chambers's own offices in the city. As he assembled his staff, Chambers reached out to Alan Court, a veteran aid professional with twenty years inside the UN who, at age sixty, was just finishing his contract with UNICEF. Court, a Briton, had begun his aid career in his mid-twenties, helping Bangladeshi volunteers inoculate the population of Dhaka against smallpox in

1973. He had since worked across Asia and Africa, often on malaria, and had also been UNICEF's director of supply, a role in which he had sourced drugs, nets, and equipment around the world. Chambers's methods appealed to Court—UNICEF had been the first large aid organization to introduce then–unheard of concepts like targets and deadlines in the early 1990s—as did the intellectual symmetry of returning to where he'd started three decades earlier: working on the eradication of a single disease. Says Court: "Joining Ray made sense. It was a good fit."[6] To Chambers, Court's unparalleled knowledge and contacts would be a big advantage. He knew who supplied what to whom in the malaria world. He knew the aid community, UN lifers and donors. He knew NGOs and volunteers and health ministers in every country in which Chambers was going to be engaged. "Having someone who can operate inside that world like Alan can, and is respected, was going to be a huge asset—not least because it would take that burden off Ray," says Basu.

Other recruits included Tim Castano as chief of staff. Chambers knew Castano from New Jersey, where Castano had worked as a speechwriter for the governor after leaving college. Soon after 9/11, while still in his mid-twenties, Castano had been appointed special advisor at the New York and New Jersey Port Authority. As well as owning and operating the world's largest airport network, the George Washington Bridge and the Lincoln Tunnel, the Port Authority owns the World Trade Center. In the years after 9/11, Castano's day-to-day work focused almost entirely on the reconstruction of the site. Dry, neat, self-effacing, and obsessed by detail, Castano would later joke that the emotive and vexed task of rebuilding the World Trade Center was handy preparation for negotiating the byzantine logistics of flying a UN special envoy across Africa.

The team was completed by Wendy McWeeny, who had advised Chambers for more than a decade at his foundation, and Sean Hightower, another New Jersey native, who took advocacy and media. After Barack Obama replaced Bush in the White House, Chambers also picked up several well-connected former presidential appointees as advisors, whom he charged with plumbing their contacts across the world. These included John Simon, former US ambassador to the African Union and ex-head of the US government's Overseas Private Investment Corporation, which drove US business investment in developing nations, and Kristen Silverberg, former US ambassador to the European Union. John Bridgeland, known as "Bridge," a lawyer and former assistant to Bush and director of his Domestic Policy Council, also became an advisor to Chambers and Malaria No More. The former head of PEPFAR, Mark Dybul, who had already helped lead a global fight against a developing world epidemic, also came on board to advise Chambers on strategy and, for a while, led the office as managing director.

Unusually for a UN office, Chambers's own foundation covered salaries and costs. Mostly he got whomever he wanted. "Ray could basically handpick his team," says Basu. "I loved the Bank—it's a pretty free place and you can say what you want—but in the end you march to the beat of the organization. With Ray, when he was trying to employ people, he would tell them: 'The one and only job you have—and you have complete freedom in this—is to hit the target. You guys have the freedom and the mandate to crack this in two years. There really are no rules.' To have the freedom to wake up every morning and know your one job is how to do better or more effectively at winning against malaria—very few people working on critical issues have that freedom or mental space. It was very different from traditional development."

The office atmosphere was also unlike any the new team had experienced. On Chambers's recommendation, the team found themselves consulting regularly with management consultants McKinsey, just as a new business would. Chambers also encouraged an intellectual free-for-all. "We'd have these meetings and just throw around ideas and debate each other about malaria," says Basu. "It's not like we were a bunch of private-sector mavericks. But we took people who understood the value of free thinking. Ray is a very organic thinker, and he would empower us to think about doing things differently—and then encourage us to actually do it differently. It'd be: 'Let's try that? Why not?' It was a start-up culture."

Chambers had his target, and he had his team. He was missing two things: a plan and money. Chambers decided both had to be in place to present to a global summit on malaria, which he had called for that year, on September 25, 2008, in New York and which was to be attended by twenty heads of state.

To construct a plan, the team decided to break down the task of eradicating malaria into separate phases. Phase I, as already announced by Ban on April 25, was universal coverage: the distribution of a long-lasting insecticide-treated bed net to everyone in the world who needed one by the end of 2010. Phase II was the end of malaria deaths by the end of 2015. Once malaria was under control and no longer a lethal threat, Phase III would be the eradication of the disease from the planet—no more malaria, ever. That, it was reckoned, would take a couple more decades and probably require a vaccine.

On the face of it, it was not a complicated plan. The technology to fight malaria was known, simple, and cheap. Universal coverage had two requirements: enough nets and good distribution. Achieving Phase II also looked simple on paper: ensuring nets were being properly used and the global distribution of diagnoses and treatment drugs. Even eradicating malaria was, in scientific theory, not hard. Vaccines were already undergoing late-stage trials. Even without them, sixty years earlier, Europe and the US had eradicated malaria by killing enough Anopheles with insecticide. Chambers liked to say that compared to other public health issues like HIV/AIDS or tuberculosis or international flu pandemics, malaria was "low-hanging fruit."

The problem wasn't the plan per se. It was the scale of it. Walk into the clinic of any doctor who stocks malaria prophylactics, and he'll show you a map of the world with the malaria hot spots colored yellow, orange, and red, according to risk. On the map, most of the tropical world—much of South and Central America, nearly all of Africa and Asia—is orange or red. In 2008, the WHO was estimating the total number of people potentially at risk from malaria at around half the world's population: 3.3 billion people in 109 of the world's 198 countries. Working on the basis of one bed net for every two people, that meant 1.7 billion bed nets. Since each net cost $10 to make and send out, that was $17 billion for the nets alone.

Even using the mythical powers of leverage, that figure was impossible. Chambers and his team quickly decided taking on the entire world was also impractical. "We couldn't be in the weeds everywhere," says Basu. But it turned out that the doctor's maps were misleading.[7] Malaria might be our oldest and biggest disease, but it does not affect the whole world equally. In theory, you can catch malaria in three continents. In practice, you are far more likely to catch it in Africa—more than 90 percent of all malaria cases occur there, and of the thirty-five countries in which the WHO says 98 percent of all malaria deaths occur, thirty of those were in Africa. In Africa, universal coverage would mean covering a far more manageable six hundred million Africans with three hundred million bed nets at a cost of $3 billion.

Chambers and his team also noted that even within Africa, the chances of illness and death rise further still once you approach the Equator. Nigeria, just north of the line, accounted for a quarter of all global malaria cases alone. This wasn't merely a reflection of Nigeria's large population, 150 million people. It was also to do with malaria's concentration. According to the then health minister, Eyitayo Lambo, across Nigeria malaria accounted for 60 percent of outpatient visits to health clinics and 30 percent of all children's deaths. "Stop and think of September 11, 2001, when 3,000 people died in one day in this country and think what it did to us," Wolfowitz had said at the White House summit. "Then imagine that it's happening every day, day after day, in Africa."[8] Like the 9/11 killers, malaria took life in pockets. In theory, that should mean it might itself be killed by focusing on a few bad places.

Chambers's team worked out that Nigeria plus southern Sudan and five other countries—Tanzania, Kenya, Ethiopia, Uganda, and the Democratic Republic of Congo—accounted for two-thirds of all malaria cases in the world and 85–90 percent of all deaths. "Well, shit," said Chambers, "maybe we focus on those seven countries, really delve into detail in those countries, and on the old 80/20 rule of business, the rest will be swept along." The WHO, whose focus was global, would ensure smaller, less malarious places were not abandoned. But by focusing on malaria in just 7 of the world's 198 countries, the UN special envoy would be hitting most of it.

So Chambers knew what to do and where to do it. On the drawing board, his team had reduced killing malaria and saving millions of lives to a logistics exercise—distributing 300 million bed nets across Africa. But they still had just a little more than two and a half years to do it, which worked out at pushing out 312,500 nets a day, every day. "This was a marathon plan, taken at a sprint," says Basu. And it was in the logistics, the team knew, that they were going to have difficulties.

In places like the DRC or southern Sudan, you couldn't just put a bed net in the mail. There was no mail. There were no addresses. There were barely any roads. Moreover, a bed net was all but useless unless it was handed out by someone who explained how to use it and how it stopped malaria. Almost every single one of Chambers's 300 million nets would have to be hand-delivered—and that to some of the most inaccessible terrain on earth.

This was hardly something to attempt alone. Chambers had long championed the merits of spreading aid beyond those who did it for a profession. Malaria, it turned out, gave him no choice. His target wasn't possible even if Chambers involved every aid worker in Africa. Malaria was literally bigger than aid. Says Basu: "We had to take malaria out of the traditional realm of the development community. We were exceptionally inclusive. We were trying to build as big a tent as possible." That meant involving private businesses, religious groups, sports teams—anyone with an interest or a presence on the ground. The response, encouragingly, was good. "They were right there," says Basu.

An unexpected bonus, Chambers's team noticed, was that the involvement of such newcomers galvanized the traditional health NGOs. "When the development community saw outsiders involved, it elevated their sense of importance of the task," said

Basu. Chambers's hustle and organizational skill, the new players he brought to the campaign, his title—all of it gave aid workers the permission, as Basu describes it, to go to work. "Most of these people are working in development because they truly want to make a difference," says Basu. "It's just that the system can beat you down. Ray provided the political cover to go for a stretch target and to break the bureaucratic glass and get the job done. It was classic leverage, what Ray's always done." Other business principles were also proving invaluable, adds Basu. "It's amazing what you can get other partners to do when you incentivize them properly, when you set a deadline. Right there, we were breaking the old mold of development. We were applying business principles to a development problem."

Even before distributing the nets, however, there was the problem of having enough to hand out. There were only four bed net manufacturers in the world. An insecticide-treated bed net costs all of $10 to manufacture and distribute, a bargain when you consider it could save two or more lives, but with the scale of Chambers's operation, that still meant $3 billion. A market of $3 billion should be incentive enough for some large-scale manufacturing. But who would pay for that? Who could?

As the newly expanded malaria world gathered for their summit in New York on September 25, 2008, Chambers had two stunning pieces of news: he had the plan, and he had the money. The detail of the plan was spelled out by Professor Awa Marie Coll-Seck, executive director of the Roll Back Malaria Partnership. If properly implemented, Coll-Seck told an audience that included Bill Gates, Bono, Gordon Brown, Robert Zoellick, and Rwanda's Paul Kagame, the plan could halve malaria deaths from one million to five hundred thousand by the end of 2010 and save four million lives by 2015. "The Global Malaria Action Plan is a milestone in the international response to malaria," said Coll-Seck. "We have had isolated accomplishments over the years, but this is the first time we have drawn together those experiences to produce guidelines to replicate success globally. Putting the plan into action must now become our number one priority."[9] The strategy was essentially an expanded version of the one drawn up by Chambers's office in answer to the single question he repeatedly asked them: "What would it take?" But crucially for Chambers's authority, Coll-Seck, Chan, and the Gates Foundation had now ensured it was endorsed by hundreds of malaria organizations and specialists around the world.

Reporters asking what all this would cost were told fighting malaria across the planet would take $5.3 billion in 2009, $6.2 billion in 2010, and $5.1 billion every year between 2011 and 2020. For Africa alone, the annual cost for delivering bed nets, insecticides, and malaria medicine was set at $3 billion, as Sachs had predicted.

The mention of money was the cue for Chambers's funders to take the podium. From 2002 to 2006, the Global Fund had handed out $2.6 billion to malaria programs in eighty-four countries. That had accelerated in the last year and a half, but Chambers still needed more. Addressing a Global Fund board meeting in April, he and Coll-Seck had thrown down the gauntlet. Unless the Fund sped up the funding—the applications process, the Fund's decision making, the disbursement of funds—Chambers said they all might as well give up now. "He spoke well," says Court. "He was very eloquent." Fund chair Rajat Gupta also urged his board to back Chambers's plan for universal coverage. Chambers was right, he said. The best way to see the best return on their billions was to spend more, faster. The board agreed.

Technically it would be November before the funds would be formally approved. But when Gupta took the podium in New York, he announced the Fund had set aside $1.62 billion in its next round of grants for malaria.

Next up was the new World Bank president, Robert Zoellick. Zoellick announced his organization was pleased with the success of its $500 million Malaria Control Booster Program. He was in favor of expanding. And while most people regarded Nigeria and the DRC as too big, too remote, too corrupt, too inefficient, and too violent to work in, the Bank was different. There was a gap, such a big one that it would wreck the wider plan if it wasn't plugged. The Bank was now putting $1.1 billion more into the fight, concentrating on Nigeria and the DRC.

That was already $2.7 billion, a stunning total. Then Bill Gates said his foundation would put $168.7 million toward vaccine development. The Corporate Alliance on Malaria in Africa, a new group of twelve companies, pledged $28 million. DfID promised £40 million to subsidize malaria drugs. The UN High Commission for Refugees chipped in $2 million for bed nets in its camps. That made $2.99 billion, so close to Sachs's target that the difference was negligible. In addition, several other donors pledged more money for the future. British prime minister Gordon Brown promised £140 million. Henrietta Fore, then head of USAID, announced the budget for the President's Malaria Initiative had been raised to $1 billion a year for five years.

Chambers secured his funding not a moment too soon. Within weeks, the financial crisis hit. "That's how close we came to not having the money," Chambers would later remark. Gupta's and Zoellick's public commitments were key. "Without those," said Chambers, "we wouldn't have the money; people wouldn't have leaned out so far." It was a leap of faith, as well, for the countries in which the campaign would be based, says Basu. They "stepped up and believed, even though they had been let down so many times before. Amazing moment."

The money was needed to make the plan work. But it also sent a message to the aid world to take Chambers seriously. "Suddenly the goal of universal coverage didn't seem so unreachable," says Chambers. Adds Basu: "When Ray began, he had none of the finance lined up. We'd put a target out there with no liquidity behind it, and that could have been just like any other UN target, which comes and goes and nobody says anything much. But we worked to unlock that money, and in five months, we'd lined up the majority of the cash. That was huge, huge, huge."

A businessman had shown that by using business methods—targets, leverage, deadlines, transparency, and more than a little Wall Street hustle—he could achieve results in development of which no development organization had ever dreamed. But drawing up the plan was one thing. Implementing it was something else.

CHAPTER 8

Gil and Belinda

It is spring 2009, and more and more businesses are joining the fight against malaria. Attracted by the newly expanded market for bed nets, manufacturers are ramping up production from five million a month at the beginning of the year to what will be an eventual sixteen million by the end of 2010. Knowles says that barely a week goes by when he is not hosting a delegation from another corporation at Obuasi, while he himself is now also expanding, setting up new malaria programs at AngloGold Ashanti mines in Guinea, Mali, and Tanzania. The Global Business Coalition on HIV/AIDS, tuberculosis, and malaria now has two hundred twenty members and its dedicated campaign on malaria, the Corporate Alliance for Malaria in Africa, which includes Bayer, Chevron, Coca-Cola, Halliburton, and Marathon Oil.

In April, a global malaria conference is held at Wilton Park in southern England, which is when I am first made aware of the campaign. Malaria, I quickly realize, is persuading the business world to behave in unusual ways, and I spend a hectic few days interviewing as many of the delegates as I can by telephone from South Africa. Richard Feachem, then the executive director of the Global Fund, tells me he is noticing "there is suddenly an increasing number of more visionary and worldly CEOs and chairmen. They say: 'We may have some direct corporate interest in engaging in all these matters.'" This emerging corporate conscience is all to the good, says Feachem, but what "sustains it, what's the engine of it" is self-interest. "If a big corporation has operations in malarious areas, it gives them a very tangible and direct self-interest to do something about the disease," he explains. "If you do nothing, two things happen: the expat staff die in significant numbers, and the local workforce, who are semi-immune, they don't die, but they have episodes that keep them from work."[1]

Some businessmen are finding malaria so compelling they are quitting their day jobs. Peter Chernin has. "As a businessman," he said at the September 2008 malaria meeting in New York, in what subsequently turned out to be his last year at News Corporation, "I firmly believe that no other cause offers the same potential return on investment as malaria." Scott Case, founder of the discount travel website Priceline.com, has also resigned from his company to become the new CEO of Malaria No More. Case says he finds the ambition of the campaign interesting. But the real attraction is in "how it's being accomplished," allowing him to continue behaving as an entrepreneur but one who now directs his energies at public health rather than personal wealth. He describes the fight against malaria as the dream start-up. "I know of no greater place that you can invest great energy, and have such a profound impact than malaria." It is, he says, "a perfect opportunity."[2]

As malaria's profile continues to rise, Chambers's campaign stays on schedule. By now I have persuaded Chambers to let me shadow his campaign, wherever it takes him, and August finds him traveling through Tanzania with WHO head Margaret Chan and Tachi Yamada of the Gates Foundation. Chambers is exactly halfway through his campaign and halfway through his nets. Revised population figures for the seven focus countries mean the campaign now has to cover not six hundred million but seven hundred million people, an increase that demands an extra 50 million nets.[3] But Chambers is still on track: the latest figures from his office show 182 million nets have been delivered, just over half of his new total of 350 million.

But there are problems. A recession in the West has cast doubt over future funds. *American Idol* has cancelled the 2009 "Idol Gives Back" for the same reason. Chan and the WHO are distracted by the possibility of an H1N1 flu pandemic. And despite the Global Fund's stated commitment to spend $1.62 billion on malaria, it is being slow to hand out the money. Alan Court, accompanying Chambers, says the Fund is taking an average of eight months to make good on a grant application it has approved. A grant of $111 million to Tanzania has been delayed for a year for want of a single signature on a single document.

As Chambers, Chan, and Yamada tour hospitals and clinics across Tanzania's business capital, Dar es Salaam, they hear a single message: give us more money. Health Minister David Mwakyusa tells Chambers the health system is woefully underfunded. He says Tanzania is dealing with ten million to twelve million cases of malaria a year and sixty thousand to eighty thousand malaria deaths, a burden that costs it 3.4 percent of GDP. He adds that the average Tanzanian has to walk five to ten miles to reach a health clinic, and there is one doctor for every thirty thousand Tanzanians. At Amana District Hospital, Alex Mwita, manager of the country's national control program, tells Chambers malaria cases there have dropped from 35 percent of illnesses in children to 7 percent. He believes his country can distribute the 21.8 million bed nets it requires to achieve universal coverage by the end of 2010. But not without more money. "It might be terrifying, but the bottom line is that our program requires more than half a billion dollars to beat malaria, and the entire health budget for the country for next year is $400 million."[4] For the years until 2014, he estimates the funding gap at $447 million.

In public, Chambers projects unwavering confidence. "We are witnessing something that will never again happen in our lifetimes: a disease that has been around for thousands of years is going to be brought under control," he tells Mwita.[5] In private, he is irritated by the constant demands for cash. "The Global Fund is cutting back. The WHO is making a new focus of health systems. The bubble of $3 billion a year—those days are over. This $447 million they want? They're not getting it."[6] He is also frustrated by the Fund's slowness in sending out the cash and uses his trip to embarrass the organization. In speech after speech, Chambers hails the "new" $111 million grant from the Fund. The Fund gets the message. Within days it pays up.

The holiday island of Zanzibar, which has a population of a million, has all but eradicated malaria. But Tanzania still doesn't feel like the focus of a frenetic, global multibillion-dollar health campaign. There is no sense of urgency. Chambers's meetings drag on. There is a disturbing amount of self-regard and intellectual showiness. Reading my notes, I realize I have summarized one speech as a meaningless sequence of aid-speak: "Capacity, resources, diversity, mission, stakeholders, targets, partners, de-

centralization, goals, investment, challenges, public-private partnerships, bridging the gap, Madam Chair, all protocol ob-
served."[7] More disturbing, the fresh tiling on the floor, the new
paint on the walls, the framed photographs commemorating earlier visits by George Bush and Nancy Reagan, all suggest Amana
District Hospital is a showpiece, that this is all a performance.
I'm not the only one becoming suspicious. "Are we seeing this
because the minister is here?" asks Chan, peering into a spot-
lessly clean dispensary.

Outside a reception for Chambers at a five-star hotel on Dar
es Salaam's waterfront, Court runs me through where the campaign stands in each of the seven target countries. Despite the delays and the lack of haste, he thinks Tanzania can still make it.
Ethiopia, after a malaria epidemic in 2003, has become the campaign's big success story and a striking example of how a good
African government needs cash but little else: twenty million bed
nets have been handed out in three years, and malaria deaths are
down by half already. South Sudan, not yet independent and
ruled by a rebel army rather than a government, is the big surprise: all their bed nets are already out, largely because millions
of southern Sudanese receive food from aid agencies—a ready-
made distribution network easily adapted to nets. Court says he
is also optimistic about Nigeria. "The country had 3 percent bed
net coverage. But they've had several massive distributions, and
now the World Bank country director is complaining coverage is
only 60 percent, so they're doing a second wave now." Such a
result in Africa's most populous country, and one of its most
chaotic, is a real boost. "Talk about suspension of disbelief,"
says Court.[8]

But elsewhere there are problems. Kenya, which had been
doing well, is now slipping. The country erupted in tribal violence

after a general election in December 2007, when President Mwai Kibaki refused to accept the opposition's victory. After months of negotiations, Kibaki and opposition leader Raila Odinga agreed to share power—Kibaki remained president, and Odinga became prime minister—but the new government is paralyzed by internal fighting and the effectiveness of the health ministry has suffered. Kenya's last four applications to the Global Fund have been rejected for their poor quality.[9] The country now faces a shortfall of thirteen million nets and a possible malaria epidemic: not only are there no new nets for villages that have never had them, there's also none for villages whose old nets have worn out. That lack of replacement nets could be a disaster. Millions of Kenyans whose immunity to malaria has never developed or has dropped away because they have been dutifully sleeping under nets are about to be naked before the disease. It is an approaching humanitarian calamity.

In the DRC, the campaign has barely started. Two million bed nets have been handed out in the capital, Kinshasa, and another 1.5 million in a single province, Equateur. But that leaves 29 million nets to go in a country five times the size of France with a few hundred kilometers of paved road, a place where the entire population of seventy-one million people can expect to contract the disease at least once a year, and a hundred eighty thousand people will die of it. Phone calls and emails to the DRC's dysfunctional government go unanswered. Chambers can't get a meeting with the shy and reclusive young Congolese president, Joseph Kabila, despite a visit to Kinshasa by Court. The Health Ministry does at least have a national plan to fight malaria. But the $962 million dollar "Plan Stratégique 2009–2013" extends way beyond Chambers's timeframe and has less than half—$440 million—of its funding in place. It is also, in any case, little more than a copy of the "Plan Stratégique 2007–2011," just with the dates changed. Even worse, many of the most malarious areas in the east of the country have, for much of the past year, been consumed by fighting between rebels and the Congolese army. Court tries to be upbeat. "The DRC is doable," he insists. The two net distributions completed were efficient, he notes. Funds scheduled for later years can be sped up. Chambers will one day get to Kabila. "It's an enormous country with an enormous need, and there are gaps," he says. "But it's not overwhelming."[10]

The biggest worry is Uganda. In the early years of the Yoweri Museveni presidency, Uganda was an aid and development darling. But as Museveni entrenched himself in power, his regime has become ever more corrupt. In 2005 Uganda received its grant from the Global Fund. Then it stole it. Three former health ministers and officials from several aid groups are now being prosecuted for corruption running to tens of millions of dollars. In the years since the scandal, the Global Fund has refused to entertain applications from Uganda and has suspended the disbursement of existing grants worth a total of $367 million. Under pressure from Chambers, the Fund has just agreed to begin releasing money again in two tranches: the first to pay for seven million nets, the next to pay for ten million. But now a new row has erupted that is delaying those seven million nets: Uganda is insisting on nets of a particular thickness, made by an African company. Given Uganda's recent history, there are suspicions of kickbacks. Unsurprisingly, Uganda is where Chambers is going next, and since I'm also heading there, to Apac, he offers me a ride and the chance of a chat.

After the serenity of overflying the Serengeti, we arrive at Entebbe airport in the evening and walk straight into a press conference. It's a weird idea—asking Chambers, Chan, and Yamada to talk about Uganda and malaria before they've even cleared immigration—but it's clear that for the Ugandan health minister, Stephen Mallinga, protocol demands a few speeches. "This is a very special occasion for us," says Mallinga. Since the minister seems fuzzy on names, Chan—looking tiny next to Mallinga's goliath frame—introduces herself and then uses the occasion to go on the offensive. "Three hundred and fifty people are dying from malaria here each day," she says. "For a government not to take action is irresponsible. The government must come up with a strategy. What are you going to do?"[11]

Mallinga beams.

A reporter asks Chambers why the delegation has come to Uganda. Chambers tries flattery. "One of the reasons we came to Uganda is that we love Uganda," he says. "Over a hundred thousand children die annually from malaria in Uganda, and they are the most beautiful girls and the most good-looking boys."

Mallinga is still smiling. Then he turns to Yamada and introduces him as "someone who represents Gil and Belinda Gates. A very important person."

Yamada, unprepared, talks briefly about successes elsewhere in malaria—Zambia, Rwanda, São Tomé and Príncipe, and Ethiopia—then hands back to the minister, who concludes the press conference with these words: "Western medicine is much more advanced than African medicine in the treatment of malaria. The question was asked: why are you coming to Uganda? It's because we are the source of the Nile. There is something about the source of the Nile which draws visitors to Uganda."

It's not a promising start, and it gets worse. The following morning Uganda's malaria community—aid workers, government officials, funders—meets at the offices of its national malaria program in Kampala. Mallinga is a no-show, as is a host of other organizations. Joaquim Saweba and Peter Mbabazi, respectively Uganda coordinators for the WHO and Roll Back Malaria, make a round of introductions so long that Chan interjects: "Cut my part! Cut my part! Go to the others."[12]

Then the presentations begin. These focus not on what has been achieved but, worryingly, what might be. By the end of 2010, says Mbabazi, gesturing to a PowerPoint chart that projects total success on every measurement of malaria, Uganda *could* have scored 100 percent across the board. Injecting a note of balance, he notes that Apac has the highest rate of malaria transmission in the world and Uganda has problems with treatment, diagnosis, and health management and frequently runs out of drugs and nets. Immediately a fight breaks out between Mbabazi and the NGOs, who accuse Mbabazi of being too negative.

Then it is time to hear from the visitors. Yamada goes first. "It's not clear to me what the actual numbers are, though what's obvious is there is a substantial gap here. What does surprise me is that if there are three hundred fifty deaths a day, or a hundred thousand a year, that would place 10 percent of all world deaths from malaria in Uganda. That is surprising and alarming."

There is an awkward silence. Saweba pipes up: "Maybe you forget to tell us what we can expect from Bill and Melinda Gates?" The room erupts in laughter.

Chambers is next. "I will be candid," he says. "We have roughly fifteen months. And we have 17.6 million nets to distribute. The relationship between Uganda and the Global Fund has not been good. You have to have tunnel vision here. You must recognize that the house is on fire. The first 7.2 million will not get ordered until August 31. That means they're not likely to be here until December. The distribution won't be done until the end of February, and the Global Fund will not have the evidence it needs to approve the second tranche until February. Does that give you enough time to place an order for the next 10 million nets and get them out? You do not have time to waste, especially with a child dying every five minutes. You just have to get this done."

There is another uncomfortable silence. Then it is Chan's turn.

"Your targets are terrible," she says. "You do not want to deliver. Why are you sitting here talking? How many children are dying as we sit here? Are you even thinking of achieving the 2010 target? If not, we can close the meeting and say good-bye. I count twenty-three organizations in the room. That means some of them haven't even turned up. Why are your measurements not up to date? What are you doing here? Think about whether this country will miss you if you disappear tomorrow. If not, that means you are not doing anything to help them. Malaria is a low-hanging fruit. If you cannot even reach out to pick it, I will close the WHO office here."

Chan finishes. Nobody wants to speak. So Chan continues. "You are all silent. Are my comments falling on deaf ears?" More deadening silence. Chan begins to lose her composure. Angrily, she brushes away a tear. "We will hold you to account on behalf of the three hundred fifty women and children who die every day here," she croaks. "I'll be calling you every week."

Graham Root, who represents a group called the Malaria Consortium, responds by first asking for the media—me—to be ejected, saying my presence is inappropriate. When the request is ignored, he tells Chan he agrees with "70 percent" of what she says and welcomes her enthusiasm. But he adds the WHO needs to clean itself up before it can think of attacking others. In Africa, he says, the WHO is "very political, run by African health ministries as a retirement fund for civil servants."

Later, as we tour a health clinic in the village of Bulima, a flea-bitten truck-stop on the main highway just outside Kampala, Chambers is still fuming. "It's delay, delay, delay," he says, "and it pisses me off, and it pisses off the Global Fund. And the one thing you don't do after the history Uganda has with the Fund is piss off the guy with the money. The ministry of health is pissing around with what type of net." "The lack of urgency is striking," I say. "But where is the lack of urgency?" replies Chambers. "We have a hundred thousand people dying every year. How much more urgent does it get?" Court joins in: "It's so stupid. They're bottom on our list of countries. And in many ways, they're much more capable of doing this than a lot of the others. It's not that they can't do it. It's that they are screwing it up."[13]

Our convoy out of Kampala has only soured the mood. We are in fifteen SUVs containing a legion of suited officials and four security vehicles in which are a company of soldiers and another of police. We drive at breakneck speed, flashing lights, sounding horns and sirens, forcing other cars off the road and scattering pedestrians. At Bulima, Chan examines the clinic's records. "Everybody recovered!" she exclaims sarcastically. "How amazing!" She asks the meaning of the ticks next to each name. A woman in a suit and diamond earrings peers at the book. "It means everybody was treated within twenty-four hours," she declares. "Amazing!" repeats Chan. It's too much for one clinic worker, Augustine Kyagulanyi, who breaks ranks. "We do not have medicine," she blurts out. "We are waiting for that. And we are not yet trained. And we do not have bed nets, or any spraying. We just send people to other health centers."

We roar through forests and over steep green hills to a second village called Balibaseka. Somehow the convoy has grown: we are now thirty-one SUVs, nine minibuses, five sedans, and an ambulance—a giant procession now carrying thirty-five smartly dressed officials, eighteen soldiers, and fifty policemen. We arrive at the village school. A crowd of thousands has been assembled. The school children perform a play about malaria, with a teacher giving a commentary on a PA system:

> There is a woman coming with her child. She is really suffering. There are a lot of mosquitoes. She is really confused. Ah, sorry! She leaves the child. The baby is crying because there are a lot of mosquitoes. The mother does not want to leave the baby. She comes back. A lot of mosquitoes. Ah, sorry! Two angels come with nets for wings. What to do? They are going to take the child and put it under the net. Wow! That's good. Now the mosquitoes are not hitting. Wow! They are really happy. That's why they dance, because they are happy. They are still happy. They are still happy. They are still happy. Because the mosquitoes are gone.

A child is pushed forward to read a short poem about malaria. ("Oh, malaria! What a deadly disease malaria is! Leading to fever, shivering, and high body temperature. . . .") Then Ugandan vice president Gilbert Bukenya, whose ancestral village this happens to be, steps forward to the microphone. "The rains are beginning, and as soon as they come, all these bushes will thrash with *Anopheles gambiae!*" he exclaims. Then he turns to his guests: "We have tried our best, but we have failed. They blame me, I am taking the blame, so I am begging. You must know the many things we need."

Chan responds by saying the play was touching. She adds: "Please do not blame him [the vice president]. It's not totally his fault. Fighting malaria is all our jobs." She announces a series of measures to help fight malaria in the area—new drugs, nets—funded by a personal $50,000 donation from Chambers. Each new gift is greeted with cheers and claps, and a chorus of drums, trumpets, and trombones. "We have done our best to respond," says Chan. "Now can I ask three things of you?" She urges the community health workers to make sure bed nets, when they do arrive, are properly used. She asks the schoolteachers to educate their pupils about malaria. And she asks the children to tell their parents to sleep under a net. After each request, she asks: "Will you do it?" There are faint murmurs of assent. The vice president returns to the microphone. "Stand up and pledge allegiance to what the WHO secretary-general is saying!" he barks. The crowd shuffles to its feet.

Later the same day we tour a factory on the edge of Kampala belonging to Quality Chemical Industries, which makes treatment drugs for HIV/AIDS and malaria. Minister Mallinga has reappeared to stress how important it is to President Museveni that a Ugandan company manufactures Uganda's drugs. Quality Chemical's chief executive, Emmanuel Katangole, says his factory can produce six million tablets a day, enough to supply Uganda and the entire Great Lakes region. Everyone thinks this is a great idea, a perfect example of a sustainable, private African business that is good for both health and development. Then Katangole ruins it. "It's our request that the WHO closes one eye and gives us special treatment," he says. Quality Chemical, he confesses, has neglected to obtain the certification it needs for the WHO to buy its drugs. Can the WHO ignore this small oversight on this one occasion? Chan is outraged. "You ask me to close one eye, which I cannot do!" she says. "WHO will never compromise on quality!"[14]

It's the end of a long day, and Chan, Chambers, and Yamada want to leave. But as they hurry for their cars, there is a chorus of loud objections. "The tree! The tree!" exclaims one man. On the edge of Quality Chemical's executive car park is a small patch of grass and along its edge is a short line of newly planted saplings. At one end, there is a hole, a fresh sapling in a bag, and a shovel. "We're not doing the fucking tree!" I hear a Western voice say. There is a scramble for the cars and a gunning of engines. "I think we are having a problem here! The tree has to be planted!" shouts an indignant suited woman whose lapel badge indicates she is from Quality Chemical. Another man shouts, "Yes, the tree has to be planted! We must have the photo!" But the drivers peel off for the exit, and we're gone.

After two days of this, I'm left wondering what the point is. As I say good-bye to Chambers that night, I ask him. "Oh, this was worth it," he smiles. "At Quality Chemical, I got the minister talking, and I asked him: 'Why do you need these particular nets? It doesn't make sense.' And he said: 'OK.'" That simple statement was enough, said Chambers. His staff could use that to pressure the minister's staff. They could take it to the NGOs and the Global Fund. Everyone could be told to get moving. In that one word, Chambers had found leverage. "The tour was worth it," he repeats.[15]

CHAPTER 9

A Big Player

ExxonMobil might have the biggest oil operation in Nigeria and now see fighting malaria as in its best interests. But the problem is too big even for an oil giant. Protecting a hundred fifty million Nigerians from malaria would not be serving Exxon-Mobil's interests; it would be bankrupting. Moreover, after half a century of drilling, Nigeria's problems have evolved from a resource curse into world record–breaking corruption and a full-fledged civil war. Fixing all that is not something an oil company is qualified to do. What small efforts ExxonMobil does make to ease tension in the Delta only underline how out of its depth it is. In October 2010, militants ambush a car carrying Lakshmi Tombush, the Indian headmistress of a school built by Exxon-Mobil at Eket in the Delta, kill her driver and two police escorts, and demand $6 million for her release. She is eventually freed after the kidnappers are negotiated down to $200,000.

But since a quarter of all the people in the world who die from malaria do so in Nigeria, the success or failure of Chambers's entire campaign depends on what he achieves there. "As Nigeria goes, so goes Africa," he says when I catch up with him in Abuja in December 2009. Chambers estimates he needs sixty-three million bed nets to protect the country. With a little over twelve months left, he still has forty-five million to go. He needs a big player. And they don't come much bigger than God.

Five months earlier, in June 2009, I traveled to Kibuye in western Rwanda with Steven Phillips, John Bridgeland, Gary Edson (now out of the White House and working for the Case Foundation), and Jim Copple, an aid consultant. The group was studying how religious aid groups tackle malaria.

Kibuye, a small fishing town dotted with eucalyptus trees spread over steep gullies dropping down to Lake Kivu, seemed an unlikely location to find a Christian assistance program. High above the town, on a spur jutting out into the lake from where you can see eastern DRC on a clear day, is a giant, abandoned Catholic stone church. A notice outside explains that in April 1994, 11,400 people were killed in and around the building. A second sign in town, outside the sports stadium, says 10,000 more died there the next day.

During the hundred days of Rwanda's 1994 genocide, Hutu militias killed around 800,000 people across Rwanda, mostly Tutsis but also their Hutu "collaborators." The area around Kibuye experienced the most comprehensive slaughter of Tutsis anywhere in the country. In Western Province, where Kibuye sits, the Tutsi population was cut from 252,000 to 8,000. When the bloodshed began in Kigali on April 7, many Tutsis in Kibuye sought shelter in the church. But on April 17, a Hutu mob threw grenades through the windows, then began shooting and hacking at the people inside with machetes. The massacre took hours. To identify anyone still living in the piles of bodies, the killers would fire tear gas inside the building and then attack anyone who coughed or sat up.

Despite being a Hutu, Father Boniface Senyezi stayed with his flock and somehow survived, hiding under their bodies. But elsewhere in Kibuye, as across Rwanda, the church was complicit in the genocide. Sixty years before, Belgian colonial pastors sowed the seeds of ethnic hatred when they divided the population into Hutu and Tutsi by measuring the width of their noses with calipers. (Hutus tend to have a flat nose, while Tutsi noses are more aquiline.) That made permanent and racial a divide that until then had been porous and determined less by ethnicity than wealth—up to that point being a Tutsi denoted enjoying a higher socioeconomic status, and a Hutu who did well could become a Tutsi. The church's guilt only deepened when the genocide started. Most Christian leaders in Rwanda refused to condemn the killings. Much of the slaughter took place in churches, where vicars and priests had initially assured Tutsis they would be safe. Some of the massacres were even led by clergy.

Kibuye, then, was an unusual place in which to found a Christian global aid project. But a mere ten years after the genocide, the most influential Christian leader in the US, Pastor Rick Warren of Saddleback Church, did just that. Warren is an evangelist but also a pragmatist; he sums up his belief system in the title of his how-to book *A Purpose-Driven Life*. The book has sold millions, and Warren draws followers from across America's races and classes. His influence can be gauged by the televised debate he hosted between Barack Obama and John McCain during the 2008 presidential campaign.

Warren's big idea is to transform all the Christian churches in the developing world into primary health care centers and all priests, pastors, and vicars, and millions of their congregants, into health workers. It sounds great in theory and looked even better on a PowerPoint presentation Warren's staff showed me at their offices in Kigali. The first slide showed a map of the Kibuye area on which the three hospitals were marked. A second slide added the twenty-five health centers. A third showed all 728 Christian churches in the area. "Even if we get just one volunteer from each church," said Eric Munyemana, Saddleback Church's representative in Rwanda, "it would be an unbelievable model."

Warren calls his plan P.E.A.C.E., with every letter standing for a remedy to each of the five "global giants" that he says afflict the developing world. P is for promoting reconciliation, E for equipping leaders, A for assisting the poor, C for caring for the sick, and E for educating the next generation. Each of Rwanda's five provinces is hosting a part of the plan, and Western Province got C, which translated to $12 million to develop health. That means fighting malaria.

"Purpose-driven" implies results. And today Rwanda is scoring such dramatic reductions in malaria and improvements in health that it is held up as an example to all Africa. But the P.E.A.C.E. plan is not part of that success. When I first visited Kibuye in June 2008, Saddleback had little to show for its four years there. The situation had changed little when I returned with Phillips and the others in 2009. Work had yet to begin on the long-promised new hospital. There was no new equipment and no new staff. The P.E.A.C.E. plan had finally trained its first group of community health workers, but they were yet to start work. "They haven't done anything," said Laura Hoemeke, director of Twubakane, a Rwandan health NGO. Another senior development worker in Kigali described the

P.E.A.C.E. plan as little more than a travel agency for rich American Christians. "Rick Warren and his people have been coming here for years," he said. "There have been hundreds of visits, and they've talked a lot, but so far there is nothing to show." Even Munyemana admitted progress was slow but added it was also steady, saying he wanted to grow an "oak tree" not a "mushroom."[1]

The reasons for the P.E.A.C.E. plan's problems were easy to understand. First, it was willfully, deliberately staffed by people who had no idea what they were doing. "One of the things that I love about the P.E.A.C.E. plan is it's a plan for amateurs," Warren told his congregation at Saddleback when he was introducing the program. "It's not a professional plan. Amateurs do it for love. In fact the word 'amateur' means 'out of love.'"[2] Professional aid workers, perhaps unsurprisingly, said that was plain dumb. "It's very naïve," said Blaise Karibushi, director of a health NGO called Access Project–Rwanda, funded by Columbia University in New York. "It takes a lot of work and planning to make development aid work. If all the churches are going to distribute drugs or diagnose disease, there are going to have to be trained people; there are going to have to be some serious logistics. It's not simple. It's certainly not as simple as Warren says it is."[3] Even the P.E.A.C.E. plan's own staff recognized the problem. Antoine Rutayisire, who was helping oversee Warren's operations in Rwanda as vice chair of the Rwandan National Unity and Reconciliation Commission, said most of Rwanda's clergy were not up to the job Warren envisaged for them. "Sixty-five percent of all pastors only have primary school education," he said. "They cannot cope with all the issues we ask of them. They just mouth some spiritual platitudes that do not inspire anybody."[4]

The P.E.A.C.E. plan had a second big flaw: it relied almost entirely on unpaid volunteers. And as Dr. Lennie Bazira Kyomuhangi, who was planning to redevelop Kibuye Hospital alongside Warren, said: "The issue of volunteerism is going to pose a great challenge for us. Most people don't believe they should do anything for free, particularly when they see millions of dollars coming in and they don't get any."[5] On my first visit to Kibuye, it struck me as almost immoral to ask people to work for nothing in one of the world's poorest countries, particularly when those doing the asking arrived in a pair of private helicopters, as the Saddleback staff did. Warren told his congregation: "If somebody calls you an amateur, you take that as a compliment. Because you're not doing it for money, you're not doing it for fame, you're doing it out of love."[6] What Warren failed to grasp is that with an average per capita income of $510 in 2009, very few Rwandans can afford to do it out of love, and most are compelled to do almost everything for money.

There is a broader problem here. By combining health and religion, Warren is mixing two things that can blend poorly. Health is about trying to build the best physical life in the here and now. Religion is about spirituality and the afterlife. By strict logic, these are competing concerns—you have to die, after all, to make the central religious journey. In development, religion and aid are also often at cross-purposes. Christian aid groups that proselytize alongside their work provoke accusations that their real purpose is not to assist people but to yoke them under an alien culture, blackmailing the poor with promises of development. Many groups admit their primary goal is not assistance. When I ask Eric Munyemana whether his priority is saving lives or saving souls, he replies without hesitation: "Saving souls."[7]

Phillips and the others leave Kibuye with mixed feelings about Warren's project. The lack of urgency is galling. Copple worries that even if the P.E.A.C.E. plan gets going, a project that relies on volunteers cannot last. And though Warren sees the Christian church as nothing but positive in Rwanda, its involvement in the genocide is a poisoned legacy that will last generations.

Nigeria is another unpromising location for a faith-based aid effort. Here too religion is known as much for its deadly violence as its pastoral care. The southern edge of the Sahara is where North African Islam meets southern African Christianity, and from west to east the encounters are often bloody. In Somalia, Islamists fight Ethiopians, whose country is home to the oldest Christian churches in Africa. In Sudan, Christians and Muslims find themselves on either side of a divide that has cost two million lives since 1956 and, in July 2011, was due to become a solid border between north and south. West Africa even has its own branch of al Qaeda, which kidnaps and executes Western tourists in Niger, Mali, and Mauritania.

In Nigeria, the green plateau that runs across the middle of the country has seen a series of religious pogroms in the last decade—Christian-on-Muslim and Muslim-on-Christian—in which more than six thousand have died. The brutality has produced hard-line sects and gangs of extremists on both sides, the most infamous of which is the Islamist Boko Haram, which stages mass attacks on Christians and security forces in support of its demand for the imposition of Sharia law across Nigeria. Also hailing from the area is the Christmas Day bomber, Umar Farouk Abdulmutallab, who tried to detonate explosives sewn into his underpants on December 25, 2009, on a Northwest Airlines flight to Detroit. Chambers visits Abuja that same month.

Days after he leaves, forty people die as an Islamic sect battles the security forces in the streets of Bauchi, three hours' drive to the east.

But linking up with religion is Chambers's only option. Business is too small to cope with all of Nigeria's malaria. The government boasts an outstanding health minister in Babatunde Osotimehin, but, beyond him, many officials are inept or corrupt. Likewise, Onno Rühl, the World Bank's country head, has adopted fighting malaria as a very personal battle—but while he has the money, he doesn't have enough people. "I don't think we have a choice," says Chambers. "I do not think Nigeria can achieve what it needs to without the leadership of the faith communities. They're essential."[8] Tom Woods is from the Center of Interfaith Action (CIFA), a US lobbying and coordinating group that is helping to organize Chambers's visit. He agrees. "The international community is scared it's going to pump $1.2 billion into Nigeria and walk away with nothing," he says.[9]

Islam and aid have a mixed history in Nigeria. In 2003, some northern state governors and religious leaders imposed a year-long ban on polio vaccinations, claiming the medicines were contaminated by Western powers to spread sterility and HIV/AIDS among Muslims. The embargo effectively stalled the entire global drive to eradicate polio. But once the imams and local authorities relented and a mass vaccination campaign was carried out with their assistance, by 2010 polio was all but wiped out.

Woods argues that co-opting religion could have similar advantages for fighting malaria. First, "you have these incredible hierarchies. You can just do things by fiat." Second, there is the sheer number of priests and imams across the country—a total of around a million, says Woods. Third, religious organizations are part of the community. "We are not going to see people having huge events in Geneva," he says. "You're going to see people who care about Nigerians every day, who are used to working around difficulties. They're already engaged; they're already administering to the poorest of the poor. We're just asking them to add this to their everyday work. It's actually amazing nobody has done this before."

For Woods, Nigeria is also a chance for religion to show its best side. The size of the country and the baggage religion carries there make it tough. But the antagonism between Christianity and Islam in Nigeria also raises a tantalizing possibility. Just as fighting malaria in Ghana resolved the resource curse, might bringing together Christians and Muslims to combat malaria offer peace to Nigeria? "It's always on our minds that we are fighting more than just malaria here," says Woods. "Nigeria has a tortured history of religious conflict and manipulation. A lot of religious people here know that, but they need a vehicle on which to collaborate. Malaria is that vehicle, something to help isolate the extremists on both sides. Hopefully Christians and Muslims will say to each other: 'I just did a training session with you last week. So I know you care about my family.'" If it works, adds Woods, the campaign will be an example to the world. "We're not doing this just because it's a good idea, or because we want to feel good. Malaria is a way for these two great faith communities to come together and solve their problems. This is the birth of something that will dramatically change the landscape of how development is delivered and sustained on this continent. It should also be a model of integrating the faith communities that can be replicated elsewhere."

To that end, Woods wants not only to prove religion's case but also to have it seen to be proved verifiably "with a rigorous monitoring and evaluation." So CIFA is mixing aid and religion *and* business by employing the consultancy KPMG to assess the campaign's performance to "world-class standards." "Our business is to translate faith into action," says Woods. "It is not our business to close our eyes and pray when people suffer." In words that echo Chambers's, he adds: "Nigeria is proof of concept."

The scale of what Chambers and Woods are attempting in Nigeria becomes apparent when they address thousands of imams at Abuja's Central Mosque. This is, Woods tells the gathering, "the largest Christian-Muslim collaboration in the history of the world." Onno Rühl adds it is also "the largest public intervention in the history of the world. Nigeria will succeed. Nigeria is the next world power, and the entire international community is with you."[10]

Chambers tries to inspire the crowd. "We are at a unique moment in time," he declares. He tells the story of Sachs's pictures of children in malarious comas. "I will never be able to get that image of those angelic children out of my mind's eye." Three hundred thousand people, mostly children, die like that every year in Nigeria, says Chambers. Seventy-five million Nigerians have contracted the disease. Malaria costs the country $10 billion a year. A third of the children in Nigeria who die in their first year die from malaria. "The eyes of the world are on Nigeria. It is the biggest country in Africa, it has the highest incidence of malaria, but it is also the country with the greatest potential. What you are doing here represents to President Obama a template that needs to be followed throughout the world. This is no longer us and them. We need to come together as one. This is the type of irrational commitment and unconditional love that you need to put an end to this disease. It's an unleashing of an army of kindness. The destiny and dignity of Nigeria's children are in your hands. I know those hands are responsible. What do I see in the distance? Children who no longer die."

It's the most moving speech I've heard Chambers give. But the imams are not listening. Chambers can hardly make himself heard above the hubbub. There is silence, however, when the Sultan of Sokoto, Alhaji Muhammad Sa'ad Abubakar, effectively the most senior Islamic cleric in Nigeria, takes the stage for a few brief words. There is silence too for the head of Nigeria's Methodist church, Archbishop Sunday Ola Makinde. "A mosquito goes to a mosque and goes to a church," says Archbishop Sunday. "A mosquito worships on Friday and Sunday. Malaria kills all of us. It is the killer of your brothers and your mother. Our business is not just to gather but to translate words into action." The archbishop sits down to thundering applause.

Suddenly it's clear how badly Chambers needs not just a higher authority, but a Nigerian one as well. He may be the UN special envoy for malaria, a friend to titans of business, and able to enlist the world's elite in his plans. (Former president Bush and former prime minister Blair will both follow him to Nigeria in February.) But in Abuja's Central Mosque, Chambers is just another white man in a suit telling people what to do.

This need to woo a Nigerian power makes sense of the zeal and flattery I have seen Chambers and Minister Osotimehin deploy in Abuja. The night before, Osotimehin told a dinner of one hundred health officials and aid workers: "We are here tonight with a great deal of hope. There's nothing stopping us now. We've learned to cede leadership to the true leaders of the country. And with the unparalleled emissaries we have now taking control of mobilizing the people, the kind of thing we see happening here now is unprecedented."

Chambers went further. "I have fallen in love with Nigeria, and I love Nigerians," he said, to broad smiles and emphatic nods around the room. "I have never encountered this type of partnership, the talent, the spirit. That does not exist anywhere else. You are blessed. If you feel the passion in my voice, it's there. This group here is about to do something that has never been done anywhere in the world: take a disease that kills a million people a year, and bring it to its knees. Nigerians are the chosen people."

When I query his effusiveness later, Chambers tells me: "In business, I have learned that if you can take a crisis or opportunity and turn it into a chance to build and move forward, the outcome is likely to be so much better than if you just criticize. Dwelling on the negative just doesn't make sense."[11]

Chambers's sweet words seem to work, at least on the Catholic archbishop of Abuja, John Onaiyekan, and the Sultan of Sokoto. Both reply that they see the malaria campaign as a natural extension of pastoral care and a way to calm tensions between their religions and avoid what Archbishop Onaiyekan calls "the two to three times a year when the mad dogs take over." The archbishop continues: "We've been able to build up the kind of organization whereby both religions are not only working together but also working with government and international agencies. That's the first time that's happening, and if it works for malaria, it should work for any other area of human development. This is open-ended. I really think we've started something here. It's like we're on an airplane on a runway gathering speed. We're about to take off." The Sultan adds that fixing malaria was restorative not only for his country but also his faith. "The more we have religiously strong people doing what is right for their country, the stronger Nigeria will develop," he says. "Coming together for a human cause is very sweet music to listen to. We are totally committed, not just to eradicating malaria but all other diseases."[12]

In private, Chambers is fretting. He tells a breakfast meeting with Nigeria's malaria community on his last day in Abuja that "this is the most impressive public-private partnership I have seen, and the results so far—fifteen to seventeen million nets delivered, with a 63 percent utilization even initially—justify the effort." But he worries about that 63 percent. "That's good for Africa, historically," he says, "but it's still unacceptable. The question is: what do we have to do to achieve this daunting and sometimes unrealistic target?"[13]

Chambers is most dismayed by Nigeria's funding problems. The Global Fund has handed out grants of $300 million, and the World Bank even more. Even after all that, Chambers's entire campaign now hangs on a shortfall of a few million dollars needed to buy the last 9.5 million nets and $1 million to pay each of Nigeria's thirty-six states to hand them out.

Onno Rühl declares: "There is no state organ in Nigeria that does not have $1 million. It's a complete joke to accept that. Anyone who tells you that is lying." The trick, says Rühl, is not to present the gap as a gap. "If you say it's a gap, they'll say: 'We have not mobilized because you haven't got the $1 million.' This is meant to be a partnership. So let's stop calling it a gap. Let's start calling it 'missing state and local contribution.' And call all the state governors together and say: 'Everyone in your state is getting two nets per household and it's only costing you $1 million.' They should go for it. That's a very good deal." Caroline Vanderick from an NGO called Support to the National Malaria Program agrees the aid world needs to turn the tables on the governors. "Our experience is that the governors will wait until the last minute," she says. "They know we will come and fix it. They know we want to do this."

After an hour of discussion, Chambers calls a halt. "We have twelve months, and it's a daunting target," he declares. "We need an irrational commitment to making this happen. We have this unique funding window, and it's not going to stay open. We have to get through that window. We have to meet these targets."

CHAPTER 10

Committed

Once again, I am flying across Africa with Chambers, along with Suprotik Basu and Tim Castano, on Chambers's plane. From Nigeria, we are heading to Nairobi. And as we cross the continent from west to east over the vast green rainforest of the DRC and the misty Ruwenzoris at the western edge of the Great Rift, the team reviews the campaign. They now have twelve months and twenty days to cover the world in bed nets. They have handed out two hundred million, leaving a hundred fifty million still to do. The deadline consumes their every waking minute. "I know the world doesn't end on January 1, 2011," says Basu. "But I'm just not concerned about that right now. Without this maniacal focus, we lose."[1]

In their effort to end malaria, the team has co-opted business and religion. They have used all the media they can, from *American Idol* to Twitter, the *New York Times* to the *New Times of Rwanda*. They have leveraged everyone they can think of too, including the White House, Bill Gates, and God. And after eighteen months, they are beginning to see results. Slowly, says Chambers, Africa is changing. "People in Africa used to accept that malaria was their lot, part of their lives. They had more children because they knew they were going to lose a few. We're now seeing that change—because nets are going out there. We've penetrated more than half the population, and it doesn't take long for word of the benefits to spread. The new dynamic is not 'It's our lot in life' but 'If *they* have a net, *we* want it too.' You can feel this new self-confidence rising across Africa." Basu says the new mood is most palpable in Nigeria. "People have been so down on Nigeria for so long. So the symbolism of Nigeria getting this right is immense. Nigeria would so dearly love to be able to say: 'Look what we did.' And other African countries are saying: 'My God, Nigeria's moving. We've got to be able to do better than that.'"

Ethiopia and South Sudan are all but done. Tanzania is now on track. Nigeria seems possible but needs constant encouragement. Progress has been, and continues to be, hard won. "Each of these countries has its own problems," says Chambers. Basu is blunter. "Every day there's another crisis," he says.

In three countries—Uganda, the DRC, and Kenya—crisis seems to be a permanent state of affairs. In Uganda, the testy relationship between Kampala and the Global Fund has not improved. Chambers is sending in a group of consultants to assist Quality Chemical to plot its future. He has also spent much of the last few months trying to persuade the Fund to ditch its two-step plan of initially distributing bed nets only to pregnant women and children under five, then following on with a second delivery of nets to everyone else. Why not cover everyone at once? The Fund's plan requires at least two visits to every affected house in Uganda. Chambers's plan would cut that to one.

But the Fund is reluctant to change at this stage, says Basu, so "we're working on getting the first two to three million nets out to pregnant women and children, and if that goes well, we'll ask them again if we can make it universal. The nets should begin arriving in January. If we can get the first three million out by March, Ray can go back to the Global Fund and say: 'OK. Now release the rest.'" It's a very tight timetable. "Uganda is still within play," insists Chambers. "But there's no room for slippage at all. You know, Protik, we should start talking to the Fund in February. These talks take a month." Basu sighs and says, "At least it's in play. When you were there in August, it wasn't even that."

The DRC and Kenya are even bigger problems. Though Chambers has identified the distribution network he wants to use in the DRC—the emergency NGOs and, possibly, the UN peacekeepers—the country is still short of the cash to pay for ten million nets. Chambers is talking to the World Bank and China about more funds, though the timetable is such that it now looks harder and harder for the DRC to make the December 31, 2010, deadline. Basu is wondering whether, when that deadline arrives in a year's time, the team shouldn't adjust their presentation of results to include smaller African countries outside the core seven that have achieved universal coverage.

Meanwhile, the catastrophe that has long threatened to engulf Kenya is now upon it. Malaria had fallen from ten million cases in 2007 to six million in 2008, saving sixty-four thousand lives and almost halving the chances of a Kenyan child dying from the disease. But since 2006, the Global Fund has rejected all Kenya's applications for funding, and a month ago it rejected the fifth in a row, saying it was worried about inefficiency. The insecticide on thirteen million bed nets protecting tens of millions of Kenyans from malaria is now expiring. Kenya needs $125 million to give new and replacement bed nets to everyone who needs one, but it has grants of only $35 million.

The World Bank, UNICEF, and other funders have indicated a willingness to step in. The Fund is also telling Kenya to appeal its rejection and come back with a better application. And Chambers is asking the Fund to take $23 million of grants it has previously approved for other types of antimalaria efforts and put that money in nets. "The Fund does feel a certain amount of responsibility," he says. "They got net coverage from 6 percent to 40 percent in the first place, and with the loss of this grant, there is a danger that slips down from 40 percent to 20 percent—plus those 20 percent will be especially vulnerable because they'll have no immunity." Still, it's a disaster. "The words 'humanitarian crisis' are being bandied about," says Castano. This is not something that can be resolved with a clever idea, like using business or religion or borrowing a prime-time TV show. With time now running out, this is going to require something less subtle. Chambers is going to Nairobi to hustle.

The next day, December 11, 2009, begins in Nairobi with a breakfast roundtable with leading Kenyan businessmen. Each delegate is handed a fact sheet entitled "Avoiding Tragedy in 2010." Encouragingly, not only does everyone in the room seem to understand the situation and how to beat malaria, but they get the economic case for it too. "If we can get people to sleep under a bed net for eight months, we'll have broken the malaria chain," says Patrick Obath, chair of the Federation of Kenyan Employers. "Business already has the distribution network to reach everyone in Kenya. Safaricom [a mobile phone operator] has agents in every corner of the country. So has Shell. So have the banks. So has Coca-Cola. And if we can get a long-lasting, insecticide-treated net into every homestead in Kenya, how many more people can we release to be productive?"

Chambers decides the atmosphere is receptive enough for him to issue a call to action. "There could be a crisis here in Kenya," he says. "The nets you distributed in 2006 are expiring. Children and pregnant women who have been covered by nets for three years have not had a chance to build their immunity. These children are now the most vulnerable in the world to being killed by malaria. You can feel the urgency. This is a critical time. We need to move quickly. Kenya did a terrific job previously. But now there is a danger of that being reversed." He also underlines the business case for fighting malaria. "Malaria costs Kenya $500 million a year. That's a big chunk of Kenya. It's in everybody's self-interest to pitch in and help. We need to use the same type of creative marketing techniques that we all use every day in our businesses. The private sector can also make sure that these applications to the Global Fund are as good as they can be. Can you envisage a public–private sector board meeting on malaria every month where you ask: 'What are the shortages? What's the budget? Where are the opportunities for new funding? How do we distribute nets?' Here in Kenya there is a lack of awareness. People don't know how they get malaria. They don't know that nets prevent it. Can Safaricom text everyone and let them know? Without that public-private partnership, I just don't think Kenya is going to succeed."

Safaricom's founding CEO, Michael Joseph, who grew the company into one of the most successful mobile companies in Africa and a world leader in mobile banking, flinches at the second mention of his company's name. "When we built Safaricom," he interrupts, "we didn't do it by coming along to breakfast talk shops. We did it by getting up off our arses. We need to come up with concrete suggestions and actions so that we don't forget everything we say here by lunchtime. I've been to too many CEO breakfasts where nothing ever happens. That's why I've all but stopped coming to them. We need to be able to come back in three months and say: 'This is what we've done.'" Chambers loves what he's hearing. "Really good energy," he says afterward as he hatches a plan with Basu to have a management consultant call all the lead speakers in the room and form a Kenyan anti-malaria business task force within twenty-four hours. "These are the guys you need to get this done."

Then the day goes downhill. Chambers takes a short ride across town to meet Public Health Minister Beth Mugo at her offices. She's not there. Chambers is shown into a waiting room. Ten minutes, then twenty, then half an hour pass. Finally Mugo—a fifty-something lady in a smart suit and coiffed hair and gold glasses—arrives, and we are shown into her office. So many of her officials come with us that we crush up against each other and jostle for seats. Chambers starts straight in. "Right now, the major funding gaps for universal coverage are the DRC and Kenya," he says.[2]

One of Mugo's assistants, a man called Sharif, interjects. "The partners' meeting will be at twelve noon," he says. "So I heard from UNICEF."

"Where did they get this?" asks Mugo. "UNICEF is not supposed to organize my time. It was always supposed to happen at twelve, but since this has happened now . . . Is Akvali here? Is Juma?"

"She is somewhere around," replies Sharif.

"I would like to have a meeting with my staff," says Mugo to no one in particular, "but since . . . "

"They are in the building," interjects Sharif.

" . . . Why don't we have our meeting?" says Mugo to Chambers. "I see the program has been reorganized. I do not know how. We are not ready for the new program. I suppose the partners keep their meeting, and we keep our meeting, which is almost now, and then we can have our other meeting, and then the press conference."

Says Chambers, "We'll just talk fast."

Mugo: "Where is Juma? What's got Juma?"

A woman, evidently Elizabeth Juma, Kenya's malaria control program manager, joins the meeting.

After a pause, Mugo tries to begin the meeting formally. "First of all," she says, "thank you for your letter . . . " Then she interrupts herself. "Do you want some tea? We are not always this disorganized. We are normally more organized. I think we can have a beautiful meeting now. Because if we go to the other meeting, by the time we get there, it will be time to come back again."

Mugo takes a deep breath and begins again. "Let me once again welcome you to this office and thank you for your keen interest in the Global Fund. I thank you also for your letter which I received in Addis. The *Lancet* magazine has confirmed our success, which is extremely encouraging. Also, we talked about the gaps. Last month the news about the Global Fund came—the health meeting here, which I opened, that's when the news came—and I had the opportunity to appeal to the chair, and they were very accommodating and sympathetic to our situation. Then your letter came, and that strengthened our case much more, and they told us they would give us five million nets through UNICEF—not UNICEF, UNITAID—and this UNITAID is meeting this week. We were with its director in Brazil, George . . . George . . . George something. Then this UNICEF is there who are the people getting the nets for us. UNICEF is looking for money for distribution. The World Bank is looking to see if there is money which can be reprogrammed. We had been thinking that there was another million that was going to come, but according to the press here, the Global Fund did not know this one million." With that, Mugo concludes. "That's the effort we have been trying to make," she says.

Juma mentions that as well as the five million nets from UNITAID (not UNICEF, she corrects her boss), a rejigging of previous grants from the Global Fund should yield money for another 2.4 million nets. In theory, the combination of these two additions should reduce the net gap from 11 million to 3.6 million. "We will probably get one million from the President's Malaria Initiative and the UK's DfID," says Juma. "So now we are missing about 2.6 million," says Mugo.

Basu speaks up. "I am quite optimistic about the World Bank," he says. "There is some room in their allocations to move things around. And the World Bank is very good at coming in and closing gaps."

Mugo turns to Chambers. "We definitely need this 2.6 million gap closed. Maybe that should be part of your campaign?"

Chambers ventures: "There is the hope or expectation that perhaps the government of Kenya would make some effort to help close the gap."

Initially Mugo seems to agree. "Yes, endemic countries should help in closing the gap. Yes, we are very committed to malaria." But then she changes tack. "We have had no real rain for the last three years. It has been drought and famine, there is a food crisis, and [as a result] we have cut money from all the ministries. So I would hesitate to think that malaria is something we can get resources for. I would hesitate to say that we can raise any money for malaria from the Kenyan government."

Chambers replies: "I think the government contribution is more symbolic than actual real money. My sense is that, as a businessman and an envoy, even if it was something in the five hundred thousand nets area . . . " But Mugo still refuses.

The meeting drags on. Chambers advises that Kenya's strategy should be twofold. Plan A: appeal the Fund's rejection of Kenya's grant application to pay for 11 million nets. Plan B: try to raise the money from other sources in case that fails. To that end, he mentions a "tacit commitment" from Safaricom to fund 1.5 million nets. Mugo muses that the Fund's five consecutive rejections of Kenya's applications are bizarre and complains the Fund has not explained its decision. Then tea arrives. "Ah!" says Mugo. "Though I do not know that we can all have tea in here. There is no room . . . "

Mugo also wants Chambers to rehearse with her their lines for the press conference later in the day. "We have a very hostile press," she says. "They must always add things that must sell newspapers. We do not want to create panic. The press knows we did not get the Fund, but they also know we are appealing, so I think we take a softer line. I introduce you. You say, 'We are concerned, and it shows that the UN takes seriously malaria in Kenya because we are here. We did not get the Global Fund, but together we are making efforts to close that gap, and we are confident we will close the gap.' You can also say something about your office and the global campaign and that you are happy to be in Kenya because we are doing a lot of work on malaria. Maybe take that line. That you are hopeful. Don't make people panic." I look over at the aide called Sharif. He's not panicking. He's asleep.

The meeting ends, and Chambers, Basu, and Castano take an elevator upstairs to a top-floor boardroom where the partners—the NGOs and foreign donors—are waiting. Chambers gives a brief outline of where the global malaria campaign stands and asks to hear what obstacles remain to achieving universal coverage in Kenya. "We really need Kenya to succeed," he says. "That's why we're on the phone and email every day." He also says that Kenya, as East Africa's economic powerhouse, should be a place where nets should eventually be sold rather than being given away. "Aid is never something we want to be permanent, something people depend on. It can get you out of a crisis and over the hill, but then the private sector has to make it sustainable."

Michael Mills, an economist from the World Bank, says the Global Fund's rejection, yet again, of Kenya's application is a deepening crisis. "We're all worried," he says. "We don't know what's going to happen." However, it was "a bit of a wake-up call, which is a good thing. We are going through a painful time right now, it's not an easy time, but sometimes you come out of those stronger. I hope you are right that we can find funding from other sources. It's going to be a big stretch."

The meeting wraps, and it is time for the press conference. The journalists are shown in. Once they have set up their cameras, Mugo kicks things off by introducing all those attending and then declares: "Today is a special day for us at the Ministry of Public Health and Sanitation." In line with the Global Malaria Action Plan, she says, "the government plans to distribute eleven million nets next year."

I glance at Chambers and Basu. There is no change in their expressions.

"The government of Kenya is committed to improving the health of its people," continues Mugo, "and Ray Chambers has been very supportive of the Kenyan government's malaria control program and our vision for a malaria-free future. Ray, we thank you for your tremendous effort and your great concern."

Chambers speaks next. "It's a pleasure to be back in Kenya at such a critical and important time," he says. "Time is getting short, but I am fairly confident we are going to achieve our targets, and Kenya plays a key role in that. The plan is to distribute eleven million nets next year, and we will see no more of these deaths. This is a disease that has killed fifty million children over time, but also one where we can see light at the end of the tunnel. If we can put $40 billion back into Africa, what other diseases can be tackled, and what other economic opportunities can evolve?"

A reporter asks Mugo why Kenya's application to the Global Fund was rejected.

"Technical reasons," she says, "which are being addressed. We are appealing, and we believe we have a good chance of succeeding this time."

Another journalist asks whether Kenya will attain universal coverage.

"We are confident that we will fill the gap," says Mugo. "If not from the Fund, then from other sources."

Chambers chips in. "The application from Kenya was an excellent application. I would have approved it, but it's not up to me. Even if the appeal does not succeed, we will raise the money to reach universal coverage by December 31, 2010. It's a little bump in the road that's occurred because of funding. But we are confident."

It's all too much for me. I walk outside into the corridor. Basu is also getting some air. "How can Mugo say she's committed to malaria?" I ask. "Half an hour ago, I saw her refuse to put even a single dollar into this."

Basu looks at me nonplussed. "What did you think press conferences were about?"

"I thought they were *based* on truth," I say. "I thought most of what was said had some relation to reality, that it was all some spun version of it. I didn't think people flat-out lied. No journalist would go to press conferences if we thought they were all just fabrication."

Basu grimaces. In truth, he finds the spectacle as unpleasant as I do. "Every time I go to a press conference, I feel I need to take a shower," he confesses.

"Then again," says Basu, "Chambers got a result." "What?" I ask. "The most important line to come out of this is that she said: 'We will get to the 2010 deadline with or without the Global Fund,'" says Basu. "They've never said that before."

It's the Newark model of accountability before the press, I realize. It's like Uganda too: in a few words, Chambers has found his leverage.

Basu says he has other good news. Because Kenya is facing a genuine emergency, Michael Mills, the World Bank economist, says Bank rules allow him to take some of the tens of millions of dollars it is meant to spend on a program called TOWA (Total War on HIV/AIDS) and reprogram it—that is, spend it on malaria instead. "They have enough to fill the gap of 2.6 million nets," he says. "Mills thinks that's the way to move this the quickest. The money put into TOWA is just not moving as fast as expected."

There is one hitch. Bank procedure demands the switch be requested by Kenya's finance minister, Uhuru Kenyatta, son of Kenya's founding president Jomo Kenyatta. We are assured of a meeting with Kenyatta at 3 PM.

Chambers, Basu, Castano, and Mugo arrive at the Finance Ministry at exactly 3 PM. We are shown into Kenyatta's office. It is empty. Once again, the minutes tick by. Soon half an hour has gone. Then fifty minutes. Even Mugo is becoming embarrassed.

"This is not a good day for Kenya," she says mournfully. Finally somebody manages to raise Kenyatta on his mobile phone.

Mugo takes the phone first and speaks. "They are saying that you, as minister of finance, will apply to the World Bank, and they will allow you to use this money for the malaria program," she says. "They will apply for another allocation for AIDS. Mr. Chambers is here, and I will put him on to say hello to you. I have already made your apologies and regretted for you—because we are sitting in your office."

Mugo hands the phone to Chambers. He closes his eyes and talks.

"If you can reallocate some of the slow-moving funds from HIV/AIDS over to malaria, then the World Bank will replenish the HIV/AIDS money," he says. "It would really help to close that gap, so that you can live up to the commitment of universal coverage at the end of next year."

"Yes . . . "

"Right . . . "

"That would be wonderful. It's clear you understand the whole situation, including the importance of covering this gap so that you do not regress and have children who have been covered no longer being covered."

"Right . . . "

"Yes . . . "

"I agree with you. We are proud of the progress Kenya has made. This reallocation would seem to be the most painless way to do this."

"That's great . . . "

"I agree with you, Minister. It seems like the most elegant solution at a very important time."

"Yes . . . "

"Thank you for this time on the phone. Sorry I could not meet you. My sense is that we will meet soon. Thank you, Honorable Minister, and I look forward to meeting you."

Chambers hands the phone back to Mugo. "He said we should move it to malaria because otherwise the World Bank will just move it to another country."

Chambers makes for the door, then turns back to Mugo. "A lot of people have talked about how Kenya is going to get close, and maybe we are going to get there in the first quarter or the second quarter of 2011," he says. "That's unacceptable. Let's turn up the burners. Let's turn up the heat. Let's get this done. I am so pleased with the progress we made here today. Let's keep it moving forward."

I ride the lift down to the basement with Basu. In minutes, Chambers and Basu will be heading back to the airport. I remark on the astonishing turnaround: from humanitarian crisis to apparent solution in a single day. "That's what Ray does," replies Basu. "No one can wheeler-deal like Ray." His phone buzzes. Basu fishes it out of his pocket and opens it. "It's a text from Alan in the DRC," he says. "Ray was right not to come. Kabila's not even in the country. Nobody knows where he is." Basu sighs. "Like I said: one crisis after another."

CHAPTER 11

The Heart of Illness

I knew the DRC. As a twenty-year-old backpacker, I'd spent two months in 1990 trying to reach a remote jungle river in the northeast of what was then Zaire, down which I planned to canoe in a dugout with a couple of friends. We spent a month crossing a few hundred miles of jungle on the backs of trucks, made it to the river, and bought our pirogue—but after a week or so, we abandoned the expedition. The heat was crushing, the swarms of little black flies were murderous, there were crocodiles in the water, the jungle was impenetrable and offered little to see, and the pirogue was no good—only half-finished, we realized, too heavy to paddle at more than a crawl, and leaking.

The DRC had become a lot more difficult since. On several return trips since arriving in Africa in 2006, I'd seen ethnic militias and the Congolese army rampage across the east of the country, raping, looting, and executing anyone who got in their way. I'd explored the crumbling, sweltering capital of Kinshasa, impossibly crowded by day and a dangerous, dingy place at night.

Outside Kinshasa, there were still very few roads. Mobutu Sese Seko, the dictator who ruled Zaire for more than thirty years, chartering the Concorde and drinking champagne while millions of his people endured disease and poverty, was gone. But he had been overthrown by a guerrilla leader, Laurent Kabila, who had proved just as autocratic and corrupt and whose assassination in 2001 had ushered into power his shy and inexperienced young son, Joseph. From 1998 to 2005, the country had been at war with itself in a conflict that sucked in armies from nine of its neighbors. The fighting killed tens of thousands, and the resulting hunger and disease killed millions more.

Even veteran Africa correspondents considered the DRC "hard-core." Lots of men with guns, few of them friendly, many fighting for control of the DRC's mineral wealth—copper, gold, diamonds, oil, cassiterite—which was often extracted by slave labor. Journalists died in the DRC. So did dreams and, it sometimes seemed, humanity. The country was littered with abandoned palm and rubber plantations and crumbling missionary outposts. Grand plans to light up Africa with hydropower from the Congo River had stayed on the drawing boards for decades. Rape was the weapon of choice for the eastern militias, the Congolese army, and sometimes even UN peacekeepers. The riches in the ground attracted the worst type of business. There was a threat of bloodshed from the moment you arrived. In the east, you came across the militias the day you crossed the border. Flying into Kinshasa airport in the west in 2008, I picked up my bag to find it soaked with blood leaking from sacks of bushmeat spinning out on the carousel.

The DRC was Chambers's most daunting challenge. Thousands of miles of jungle, tens of millions of people, with nothing connecting them but footpaths and rivers. This was the route—by barge, dugout, bicycle, and finally porters—down which thirty-two million bed nets would have to travel. In 2008, I'd experienced one of the more remote areas of the DRC's interior while on assignment to observe the creation of a new wildlife sanctuary for the bonobo, a cousin of the chimpanzee. I'd traveled to central DRC with a group of primatologists by a tiny private charter plane. After several hours flying over unbroken jungle, we touched down on a grass strip from where the only car around—a wrecked, doorless jeep—had taken us for three days down a bicycle track to the bonobos. After a few days, the plane's pilot, who had promised to pick us up, radioed to say that the country had run out of aviation fuel and he was unable to fly. We eventually made it out by tying three dugouts together, strapping an outboard to the back of one, and coasting for six days downriver until we reached a town with an airport. The whole trip cost several thousand dollars.

All that to visit one place. Chambers's campaign had to get everywhere in the DRC—because malaria was everywhere. The DRC government estimated its people suffered between sixty and one hundred million cases of the disease a year, which resulted in a hundred eighty thousand deaths. Out of all child deaths, 39 percent were from malaria. Dr. Benjamin Atua Matindii, head of the DRC's malaria program, told me in June 2009 that just 10 percent of children with malaria and 7 percent of pregnant women received treatment, while bed-net coverage was 6 percent for children under five and 7 percent for pregnant women.

As it was across Africa, malaria was a prison for millions of Congolese, trapping them in suffering and poverty. But this particular prison was one of the most remote in the world, and many questioned whether it was even reachable, let alone somewhere a jailbreak could be engineered. Readying a national bed-net distribution would take nine months. Transporting millions of nets upriver by barge from Kinshasa and then across the country would take three more months. "Can you fix the DRC?" asked Marcel Tanner of the Swiss Tropical Institute. "We do the best we can, but anyone who speaks about elimination in the DRC is seriously naïve."[1]

Chambers's team understood early on that "in the DRC," as Alan Court said, "we needed proof of concept. We had to show that it was doable."[2] On the ground, pessimism and apathy affected the effort from the start, says Basu. "The DRC's one of those places where you cannot get anyone to do any forward planning. They are so used to unmet promises of aid and development that unless they know things are on their way, they're just not going to get going."[3] Raising the stakes further, Tanner said that without tackling malaria in the DRC, Africa itself would never be rid of the disease. "This is a reservoir of malaria at the center of Africa," he said. "And it's huge."

It wasn't all hopeless. NGOs in the DRC had run effective campaigns for vitamin A shots and antiworm medicine and against river blindness, even during the years of fighting. Three times—in 2000, 2001, and 2002—the soldiers had declared a cease-fire for a week to allow for a national polio vaccination. In 2008, the American NGO PSI (formerly known as Population Services International) distributed two million bed nets in Kinshasa. That operation was, says Basu, "a nightmare": Kabila's opponents first accused him of trying to buy off voters, then spread rumors that the nets actually caused malaria. But the nets had gone out.

A second small distribution in 2007 in South Kivu, on the edge of the DRC's wars, saw net coverage in the area rise to 45 percent and child mortality drop 15–20 percent. In 2008 a third handout of 1.5 million nets had gone ahead in Equateur, through which I had traveled to see the bonobos. "All those distributions went incredibly well," says Court. "It was hellishly complicated to organize, but the nets were extremely popular, and the usage rate was incredibly high."

Encouraged, the Global Fund in 2008 set aside $150 million for a bigger net distribution in the DRC, including more than five million nets handed out by UNICEF in two more provinces: Maniema in the center and Orientale in the northeast. The operation was slow—the nets took nearly a year to arrive—but the distribution went ahead in 2009 through missionary groups, NGOs, and community organizations and was successful. By then other funders were also stepping in. The World Bank added another $60 million. USAID announced it would pay for two million nets in the southern province of Katanga; it would distribute them using the DRC's creaking railways.

In Kinshasa in June 2009 I met Patrick Mullen, a World Bank health specialist. Just getting any bed nets out at all in the DRC had been a "huge boost," he said. "There's now a real potential that we can achieve this massive program," he said. The deadline of the end of 2010 looked extremely difficult, he added, but then nothing in the DRC was ever easy. "We've proved it is feasible to do these things. It's a logistical challenge, sure, but UNICEF and PSI are very good at meeting that. They've done Equateur, one of the most difficult places on the planet—no roads, just jungle and river, and some of the poorest people anywhere in the world. Given the funding, this can be done in the DRC."[4]

Paradoxically, Mullen added, the harshness of the DRC—the lack of development, the breadth of poverty, the absence of almost anything resembling government service—was in some ways an advantage. That environment had produced a resilient population used to taking care of their own health and paying for it. That, in turn, had attracted the DRC's professional class. As Mullen described it, health was one of the DRC's very few "revenue-generating activities." "There is a surplus of trained nurses and even overstaffing in hospitals in some areas," he said. "Everybody wants a piece of the business, and it's good business: the DRC's never going to run out of sick people." That made distribution easier, said Mullen. In the province of Katanga, aid workers had carried out an experiment with incentives for health workers: subsidizing drug prices to allow more patients to buy their own drugs. "The subsidy worked," said Mullen. "Utilization of drugs shot up, and without the whole rigmarole of building a health center and training people. Just cash, used well, can make a difference." "From the point of view of the antimalaria campaign, even the DRC's wars hadn't been all bad," said Mullen. Parts of the humanitarian effort that accompanied them had been adapted to form a rudimentary health system.

So there was hope. But there were problems too. The government wanted to take control of the malaria fight but was in no position to do so. "The government's capacity problems are the reason the aid groups were required in the first place," said Mullen. "They want to focus on inputs—the money—rather than results. They want to centralize procurements [buying nets and drugs], but procurements take forever in Kinshasa. The government has had to repay money to the Bank that was not spent at all. And, of course, we're very concerned about corruption."

Sure enough, the next year, 2010, the World Bank suspended all funding to the DRC when the government sold a $20 million gold mine the Bank owned to the Chinese. Chambers met Bank president Robert Zoellick, with whom he had now developed a close working relationship. Zoellick duly made an exception for malaria. "Bob Zoellick put out the message: 'Stop everything in the DRC, but I want my malaria project to go ahead,'" says Basu. "Bob's leadership pushed that through." On April 25, 2010—World Malaria Day—the World Bank even raised its funding for net distribution in the DRC by another $100 million, enough to pay for the last of the thirty-two million nets. The money was in. There was not a day to lose, but Dr. Benjamin was adamant the DRC would make the end-of-year deadline. "It's still possible," he insisted.[5]

CHAPTER 12

Buzz

The slow progress of the campaign in Uganda, Kenya, and the DRC was one reason to worry. Elsewhere, I wondered if the campaign was growing too big, too fast. I saved a clipping from a Kenyan newspaper on September 23, 2009, that I found particularly striking.

POSH'S RING CREATES BUZZ

Victoria Beckham created a buzz for a life-saving charity on Tuesday—by showing off a £15,000 jeweled ring as she flew in for London Fashion Week. Posh is backing Malaria No More UK by wearing the ruby and diamond encrusted mosquito ring which will raise money for the campaign. She was seen wearing the item—created by designer Stephen Webster—on her right thumb as she touched down at Heathrow on Tuesday morning. Beckham said: "It's a fabulous statement piece and I've loved wearing it. It's inspiring to see designers like Stephen working the power of fashion to save lives. I'm crossing my fingers this collaboration will generate loads of buzz." Her ring is made of rhodium-plated white gold set with ruby cabochons, white diamond wings, a silver diamond tail and a black diamond band. Retailing for just under £15,000, it will be auctioned off by MNM with all proceeds from the highest bid going to the charity . . . Victoria is mom to Brooklyn Joseph, 10 1/2, Romeo James, 7, and Cruz David, 4 1/2, with husband David Beckham.

I had other examples. On July 8, 2010, the eve of the soccer World Cup Final, I attended a concert at the Coca-Cola Dome on the outskirts of Johannesburg. Star performers were the tenor Andrei Bocelli and Canadian rocker Bryan Adams, who performed a duet of *Yesterday* as a finale. The event's sponsor was United Against Malaria, a soccer-related coalition of malaria groups that tries to raise malaria's profile through the sport. During the concert, advertisements and slogans on giant overhead screens drove home the message, as did guest speakers. At one point Cameroon's goalkeeper appeared on stage and announced: "It takes a team to score victory. Help us build the strongest team ever!"

I watched the show from a VIP area, picking at sushi and sipping flinty white wine. With me were representatives from most of the world's malaria organizations, such as Malaria No More, the World Health Organization, and UNICEF. There was a lot of networking and a fair amount of drinking. Everyone had dressed up for the night, and smart young women in black with clipboards kept checking my ID and telling me I was standing in the wrong place or needed to be quieter or had to meet someone else on their list.

And as the evening wore on, I began to feel distinctly queasy. Sashimi and Sauvignon Blanc don't mix well with disease and destitution. With every sip and every bite, I realized, we were consuming money intended to save lives. Hundreds of thousands more dollars would also be spent when the people around me claimed days of expenses for food, international travel, and hotels from their own malaria organizations. And I started to wonder: were we getting more out of this than malaria? What about the celebrities, who were appearing before a global television audience? *American Idol* had given malaria a whole new profile. But was I alone in feeling there was something not quite right about Victoria Beckham's work with rings? Did fashion really have the power to save lives?

There was certainly something inappropriate about a £15,000 jewel-encrusted mosquito ring. Malaria was a disease of poverty. The ring was a dazzling reminder of the global inequality that ensured malaria endured. It suggested Beckham knew little about malaria. Such ignorance was the main reason Marcel Tanner at the Swiss Tropical Institute had little time for celebrity campaigners, a group in which he now placed Jeffrey Sachs. "If you have Sachs and Bono, it's a problem," he said. "It's helicopter action. The helicopter lands, and there's lots of dust. But when the helicopter goes, the dust remains." Tanner said high-profile campaigners "don't get a lot of dirt on their shoes. That's very important—it helps a lot. You have to see reality, what malaria means, how people interact, how hot the sun is. I get nervous people aren't in touch with reality. I start asking them: 'Friends, do you understand the life cycle of malaria?'"[1]

There was also the question of who benefited more from the publicity: the campaign or the celebrity? In the pictures that accompanied the Beckham story, the ring could scarcely be seen. Likewise, in early 2009 the American actor Ashton Kutcher was dutifully sending out Twitter messages about malaria every day, but as Kutcher's following soared, the malaria message was eclipsed by a new story: who, between Kutcher and CNN, would be first to have a million Twitter followers?

Another star involved in the campaign was the British tennis player Andy Murray. I emailed him to ask whether he thought celebrity endorsement did any good—and if it did, for whom? I received a sincere and well-intentioned lecture in reply. Murray said that his role was "to help raise awareness about what needs to be done" and described "an unforgettable day at Wembley Stadium," when he played tennis with David Beckham over a giant net made out of mosquito netting. "We also visited the former Prime Minister Gordon Brown and hung a mosquito net over the iconic door of Number 10 Downing Street," he wrote. "The point was to show the vital need for nets in Africa. Meeting these goals would transform the African continent saving literally millions of lives. Stakes don't come much higher than this."[2]

Murray was right on message. But the questioned remained: why did it take a tennis player to sell it? Sarah Kline, who runs Malaria No More's London office and manages the involvement in the campaign of the Beckhams, Murray, and others, said my concerns were misplaced. If Beckham or Kutcher or *American Idol* received more coverage than malaria, she said, that was just the way of the world. Stars didn't need malaria to make them famous. It was the other way around. "Victoria comes to London Fashion Week every year, and what she wears as she comes through the airport is a huge event," said Kline. "We chose that moment for her to wear the mosquito ring and that picture went to almost every newspaper in the world—and every report talked about malaria."[3]

It was true that celebrity involvement in a campaign was rarely selfless, said Kline—"Managers will only let their celebrities do something that works for them"—but this was self-interest that helped. Celebrity endorsement only worked if it fit a celebrity's image, reflected their interests, and complemented their profile. Otherwise, it wasn't credible. David Beckham was believable as an ambassador for UNICEF because "he has kids—those are his interests." For Murray, "it's about nets, something he works with every day." She continued: "Victoria Beckham is a fashion icon, and we were trying to sell replicas of that ring," she said. "We're not asking her to be a scientific expert. That wouldn't be credible. But if she wears a new ring and talks about fashion, then that has authenticity. That's who she is."

This was classic leverage, added Court: playing different elements off each other to create a bigger whole. It was something UNICEF understood half a century ago when it employed Danny Kaye and Audrey Hepburn as spokespeople. "Celebrities leverage not just the media and, through them, the general public, which in turn influences politicians and legislators and thus policy. They also leverage corporate and aid agency leadership."[4] Chambers was convinced there was a strong link between celebrity involvement and influencing Capitol Hill. It was a politician's job, after all, to respond to the popular mood.

And the influence *was* plain to see. There was the huge audience attracted by "Idol Gives Back" and the tens of millions of dollars it raised. Likewise, when Kutcher reached a million followers on Twitter, he donated enough money for 10,000 nets—something that inspired his followers to give funds to buy a further 79,724. Imagine that effect two hundred times over, said Chambers. "We've got two hundred people—from Queen Rania of Jordan to Bill Gates to Shaquille O'Neal—mentioning malaria at least once a month on Twitter or Facebook. Combine all their followings, and we're reaching two hundred million people."[5]

If there was something uncomfortable here, Kline argued, we should look to ourselves. The problem wasn't Victoria Beckham. The problem was that we needed her—and Ashton Kutcher and Andy Murray and Bryan Adams—to make the poor world interesting. In Britain, about 10 percent of the audience cares about international development, said Kline. "The other 90 percent don't read international development news, but they do consume celebrity magazines and reality TV. So that's what we use."

CHAPTER 13

Trade Not Aid

If there were pros and cons to mixing celebrities and malaria, the problems with the campaign's burgeoning rank and file were less ambiguous. In November 2009, a month before Chambers met Mugo in Nairobi, I attended a weeklong conference for malaria scientists in the city. So did around two thousand other delegates, most of whom had flown in from around the world. For a week, in between shopping trips and dinners in their five-star hotels, they discussed ways of preventing and curing a disease that has been preventable and curable for more than a century. This was an old aid flaw writ large. There were now thousands of people working in malaria—development specialists, scientists, researchers, academics—not because they were expert in it but because that was where the money was. Everyone proposed never-ending assistance programs. No one was planning on going out of business any time soon.

To be fair, there were some innovations. Several groups of scientists were working on different vaccines. One company was proposing using insecticide-treated wallpaper instead of nets. There were discussions about rising mosquito resistance to different pesticides and the malaria parasite's varying resistance to different drugs. But in paper after paper, the scientists proved—at length and in a hundred different scenarios—what we already knew: bed nets kill malaria, so do sprays, and antimalaria drugs can treat it. At the conference, Tim Wells, chief scientific officer of the Medicines for Malaria Venture (MMV), was as mystified as I was. Fighting malaria was no longer "about science," he said. "It's about people. It's about working out why people are not being treated with medicines or do not have a bed net. It's about how politicians tick." I also caught up with Brian Greenwood. As he surveyed hundreds of delegates crowding the conference coffee shop, he remarked: "You have to ask: 'Is this whole thing getting out of hand? Is it getting too big?' And the answer is yes, I think it probably is."[1] Marcel Tanner worried whether quantity was at the expense of quality. "Of course, it's good to have more people," he said. "But sometimes it's too much. It's overkill."[2]

And if there were too many of one sort of delegate, there were not enough of another. You could spot the problem simply by studying the list of scientists and researchers in Nairobi: plenty of Westerners, plenty of Africans working for Western NGOs, but almost no one from an African government. With all these thousands of outsiders working on malaria, why should they bother?

As I watched the malaria campaign grow into the world's biggest aid drive during 2009 and 2010, the same doubts kept coming up. Was this finally aid that worked? Or was the malaria campaign making the same mistakes of all big aid? Nairobi suggested malaria groups were as wasteful as any other. They were blind to the perennial aid flaw: how removing the responsibility for looking after a people from the leaders of a village—or a town or a country—hurts their ability ever to do so. Skills are lost, duties forgotten, and a dependency created. Short-term success is overshadowed by long-term failure.

Money for malaria came from the West, and it made sense for Westerners—celebrities or others—to make the pitch for funding. But when implementation was in Africa, it had to be Africans who led it. And yet many African governments were relying on outsiders to fix the disease. For foreigners to come galloping to the rescue was fine in the short term, when hundreds of thousands of deaths demanded an overwhelming emergency response. But the long term demanded passing on the skills to fight malaria; at the very least, it prohibited sidelining African governments.

Basu reckoned elimination would take three to four rounds of nets and spraying, rising to six or seven—a generation—in the most malarious places. What would happen when the world found another cause? The normal modus operandi of foreign aid—short-term, large-scale interventions followed by an equally rapid tailing off—suggested foreigners would not stay the course. Could that be changed? Would Africa take over? Or would malaria rebound once again?

Of all the problems his campaign faced as it entered its final year in 2010, the question of sustainability preoccupied Chambers. The problem was twofold. There was the pace of the campaign. "We've run this like a political campaign," said Basu. "But you can't operate like that forever."[3] And while their spectacular successes suggested they were the right people to run the initial campaign, durable accomplishment would require Africans to take over. Sachs had shown achievements in health and economics reinforce each other. The most developed countries, and those growing fastest, should also be most capable of fighting malaria. "Ultimately, this is about economic development," said Basu. "To truly end malaria, you grow out of it. That's the only way it's sustainable. Africa can't stay on the donor dole forever." So had Africa been given enough of a kick start to be able to start fighting malaria by itself? Could it finally begin climbing its own virtuous circle of development?

The surprising answer to these questions was: possibly. And once again, the hope derived from business. Today Africa is more a destination for business than for aid. War and dictatorships are down. Democracy and economic growth are up. Inflation and interest rates are in single digits. From 1980 to 1994, Africa's economy shrank by an average 0.2 percent. Since then, annual economic growth has averaged 2.3 percent and is rising steadily. African growth was projected to be 5 percent in 2010 and 5.5 percent in 2011.[4]

In 2006, according to the Organization for Economic Cooperation and Development, foreign investment into Africa reached $48 billion, overtaking foreign aid for the first time and reflecting a quadrupling of foreign investment in Africa since 2000.[5] That gap has only widened since: in 2010 business investment into Africa more than doubled aid.

Sub-Saharan Africa today resembles Asia in the 1980s. In an article for the online journal allAfrica.com in February 2009, Oxford University economist Paul Collier and US presidential advisor on Africa Witney Schneidman noted that the continent now offers the world's highest rate of return on investment. "Africa, usually the poorest performing region in the world economy, is now likely to be among the best-performing," they wrote.[6] Stephen Hayes, president and CEO of the Corporate Council on Africa, told me, "Africa offers more opportunity than any place in the world."[7]

Perhaps the most compelling evidence that Africa is now open for business is China's new love of it. China doesn't do aid; it does business. While the old superpowers still agonize over Africa's poverty, the new one is captivated by its riches. Trade between Africa and China has grown by an annual average of 30 percent in the last decade and topped $108 billion in 2008. Today the Chinese are pumping oil from Sudan to Angola, logging from Liberia to Gabon, mining from Zambia to Ghana, and farming from Kenya to Zimbabwe. Chinese contractors are building roads from Equatorial Guinea to Ethiopia, dams from the Congo to the Nile, and hospitals and schools, sports stadiums and presidential palaces across the continent. Where they are not digging or building or farming, the Chinese are buying: acquisitions range from a $5.5 billion stake in Africa's largest bank, Standard Bank in South Africa, to a $14 million investment in a mobile phone company in Somalia. China is becoming part of the African fabric. Chinese knickknacks dominate street markets from Mauritius to Mauritania, Asian fusion is the fashion in restaurants from Antananarivo to Abuja, and airports across the continent sell *China Daily* and cheap Chinese cigarettes. Dambisa Moyo, author of *Dead Aid*, says anyone who needs convincing on Africa should ask themselves if they are convinced by China. "Because if you back China, you're backing Africa."[8]

The growth is heralding a new mood of self-sufficiency. The African Union, formerly little more than a talk shop for dictators, is now vocal about how Africans should take care of

African problems. And it is backing that sentiment with action. Rather than rely on the UN or other foreigners, AU mediators took the lead in messy African crises the rest of the world preferred not to touch: in Kenya during the postelection violence of 2007; in Sudan, which split into north and south in 2011; in Somalia, where an AU force in Mogadishu was also protecting the government against an Islamist insurgency; and in Côte d'Ivoire, where a president defeated in an election in late 2010 refused to step down.

Aid was also attracting ever more criticism from within Africa for, as the critics saw it, unnecessarily supplanting governments. Rwandan president Kagame was the most prominent of aid's detractors but far from the only one. His views were widely shared by a new generation of antiaid Africans who had had enough of foreigners telling them what to do. When those outsiders were Western celebrities, distaste became detestation.

In Ethiopia in 2007, I met Mulugeta Aserate Kassa, who was organizing that country's millennium celebrations in 2007. (Ethiopia uses a modified version of the Julian calendar, which is almost seven years later than that used by the rest of the world.) He had asked the Black Eyed Peas to headline a celebration concert. I asked whether he had invited Bob Geldof. Mulugeta, a distinguished looking fifty-six-year-old with an exemplary Oxford English accent to match his pinstripe suit, exploded. He was incandescent about criticism Geldof had made of Ethiopian prime minister Meles Zenawi, telling Zenawi to "grow up" and "behave" when Ethiopian police shot dead hundreds of opposition protesters in 2005. "People like me are still absolutely furious about what he said," said Mulugeta. "What right has he got to be so paternalistic as to tell African leaders how to behave? My God, if he wants to ever come back here, he'll have to apologize. Nobody denies we have had famines and drought. We have been through that. We feel it in our bones. But we have picked up the pieces."[9]

Similarly, in 2009, I interviewed Andrew Rugasira, the CEO of Good African Coffee, a Ugandan coffee company he set up in 2004 to supply British supermarkets from Kampala under the motto "Trade, Not Aid." For Rugasira, aid not only "undermines the creativity to lift yourself out of poverty" but is also humiliating, even racist. "Aid undermines the integrity and dignity of the people. It says, 'These are people who cannot figure out how to develop.'" Like many of his peers, Rugasira was especially infuriated by Western celebrities championing aid. "African governments become accountable to Western donors, which is bad enough," he said. "But Africa also finds itself represented not by Africans, but by Bono and Geldof. I mean, how would America react if Amy Winehouse dropped in to advise them on the credit crunch?"[10]

And if some Africans did not want aid, others were demonstrating why they didn't need it. In Kenya, Michael Joseph's Safaricom had given tens of millions of subscribers access to bank accounts, money-transfer loans, and credit cards by linking up with a bank and allowing subscribers to send each other money by text message. At a stroke, Safaricom not only created the world's first mass mobile banking service but gave economic growth the kind of boost development specialists can only dream of.[11]

In 2009, I came across a manifestation of African self-sufficiency that had the potential to change the entire continent. The consensus among climatologists and development specialists was that climate change was the biggest challenge facing Africa.

It was pushing the Sahara south, ruining farmland, raising hunger, and likely, so they said, sparking famine, war, and the migration of tens of millions of refugees. The UN Food and Agriculture Organization says that on the Sahara's southern edge, an area the size of Somalia has become desert in the last fifty years. The UN Environment Program reports that fourteen African countries currently experience water scarcity or stress and that number will rise to twenty-five by 2025. In a September 2008 report, the UN Convention to Combat Desertification (UNCCD) reported 46 percent of Africa was threatened by land degradation.

The coming crisis is predicted to have a massive human cost. As the number of farms shrink, the number of mouths to feed will grow—the Sahel (the transition zone between the Sahara and the lush farmland to its south) has some of the highest population growth rates in the world. Food prices are also likely to rise, and with them poverty and disease; mosquitoes and locusts both thrive as temperatures go up. The Intergovernmental Panel on Climate Change predicts that by 2020 climate change will put at risk of hunger eighty million to a hundred twenty million people, of whom 70–80 percent would be Africans. In a May 2005 study, Oxford and Duke University environmentalist Norman Myers calculated sixteen million "environmental refugees" in Africa in 1995 and predicted that number would double by 2010. In April 2007, the UN Security Council held a debate on how climate change, by exacerbating poverty and friction between rival tribal groups or even countries, can start wars. UNCCD executive secretary Luc Gnacadja concludes climate change is making desertification "the greatest environmental challenge of our times" and calls the effort to reverse it an attempt to "help ensure humanity's survival."[12]

By now I was familiar with aid world hyperbole. I expected the reality was less sensational. What I did not anticipate was that it would be the exact opposite. Flying into Niger in late 2009, I'd noticed strange shapes appearing on the desert floor below. They stretched in ordered rows to the horizon. At a few hundred feet, they revealed themselves as the shadows of millions of trees.

Further investigation revealed farmers were digging holes and ditches shaped in moon crescents and square brackets and erecting low fences out of stones, deadwood, and brush to catch drifting soil. These obstructions were keeping the dirt stationary long enough for it to catch water and insects, germinate seeds, catch more soil, allow the farmer to add manure—and gradually become small, narrow fields.

Since work began in the 1970s, the fields have grown. Some have become woods. Instead of being sucked downward into the spiral of desertification, they have kick-started a new virtuous cycle of life. Grassland and trees trap the desert. Fruits and vegetables grown in their shadow provide food for people and animals. Animals produce manure for the soil, creating bigger, healthier fields. Rainfall has increased. Hunger has fallen.

On a trip to Niger in 2004, Chris Reij, an environmental scientist with the University of Amsterdam, found the new green cover had lowered the average daytime temperature from 113 degrees Fahrenheit to 104 degrees Fahrenheit. Reij asked the US Geological Survey to take some satellite images of Niger, and he then compared them to ones from 1975. A data-driven scientist, Reij cautioned himself not to get carried away. "I thought maybe they had re-greened a few hundred, perhaps 1,000 hectares," he says. When the results came back, he found "they'd re-greened 5 million hectares. That's 200 million new trees—20 times the number that had been there before." In the wood they produced, the food and animals they allowed to grow, the lives they saved, Reij estimated the economic value of the trees at €200 million. That was enough to feed 2.5 million people. What's more, in Niger, the Sahara was no longer spreading south. "It's the biggest environmental transformation in Africa," Reij said.[13]

What had driven the change? Tens of thousands of small farming businesses. Niger suffered a drought from 1968 to 1974 in which more than a hundred thousand people died. After initially trying to decree environmentalism by law—renaming Independence Day, August 3, "Arbor Day" and ordering every citizen of Niger to plant a tree on the anniversary—the government tried green economics. In 1993, the state allowed farmers to own, buy, and sell their own land for the first time. This initially caused some violent disputes. But it also created opportunity. Farmers could now plan on long-term returns. Years of labor on a ditch, known in Niger as *zai*, became not just socially worthwhile but personally profitable. Returns were good. Reij says each hectare of rescued land brought in an extra $70 per head in a country where, according to the IMF, average per capita income was $185 in 2010. Farmers who previously harvested one crop from every four sowings were now reaping each time they planted. Collecting firewood would take minutes instead of hours, and there was often a surplus to sell. Farmers even began buying new patches of desert to rehabilitate and expand their fields. Trees, soil, and water became capital. Fighting climate change became development. "What's more," says Reij, "most of it didn't cost anything."

The implications for desertification, and global warming, are immense. So are the lessons for Africa. With no assistance at all, hundreds of thousands of Africans living on the edge of the Sahara are turning back the desert. Niger's success is now being replicated in Mali, Burkina Faso, and elsewhere. In the northern Ethiopian district of Tigray, farmers have regreened a million hectares. An eighteen-year project in Tanzania's Shinyanga region, just south of Lake Victoria—a place nicknamed the Desert of Tanzania until recently—has seen three hundred fifty thousand hectares replanted, making 2.8 million people around $170 a year better off, according to a study by the International Union for the Conservation of Nature.

Ever on the lookout for opportunities to use leverage, Chambers decided to capitalize on Africa's new mood of self-determination. He involved African celebrities, such as Youssou N'Dour and the South African singer Yvonne Chaka Chaka. He championed the Tanzanian bed-net manufacturer A to Z and sent consultants to assist Quality Chemical Industries to become operational in Uganda. And he drew in Africa's governments by creating the African Leaders Malaria Alliance (ALMA). John Bridgeland first raised the idea with Kagame during his trip there in 2009. By the end of 2010, ALMA was up and running, with Tanzanian president Jakaya Kikwete as its first chair, former World Bank vice president for human development Joy Phumaphi as its executive secretary, its own offices across the continent, and thirty-five African heads of states as members. "We're trying to hand more and more of what we're doing off to ALMA," said Basu in late 2010.

Africa would still rely on outsiders to fund the fight against malaria and even, at least initially, to implement it. But under ALMA, it would increasingly direct it. Basu said ALMA was already proving itself more effective at influencing African governments than any foreigner in a suit. "Leverage works well for us in terms of fund-raising and advocacy," he said, "but we have significantly less impact at the country level. That's where ALMA comes in. The battle against malaria must be led by African heads of state. Inside ALMA, they exercise peer-to-peer leverage. If we can get this right and have ALMA function as a true collective, it will be a total shift in how we do development and could be one of the greatest legacies that Ray could leave." Chambers said he was now telling every African president he met: "We've given you a turbo boost. And you're all adamant about self-determination. Well, what greater example of where you can take that than by saying 'This is our fight. Here is our path out of aid'? Go for it!'"[14]

Chambers was under no illusion that handing off the campaign to ALMA would be easy. "It's perhaps the most ambitious thing we have to do, and we expect a lot of skepticism," said Basu. The resistance from the aid community, used to being in charge, would be particularly firm. But Chambers was resolute: "I don't have a career in development ahead of me. I can say things others do not want to hear."

There were also doubts about how well ALMA would function. Africa was increasingly ruled by a higher caliber of leader, such as Jakaya Kikwete in Tanzania or Ellen Johnson Sirleaf in Liberia. Above all, Ethiopia proved that good African leadership was the key to killing malaria. The Ethiopian health minister, Tedros Adhanom Ghebreyesus—who replaced Rajat Gupta as chair of the Global Fund in July 2009—delighted Chambers on a visit to Addis Ababa by telling him, "My government has prioritized malaria. Even if the donors leave tomorrow, we will pay for this."[15]

But Chambers's time in Kenya, Uganda, and the DRC had shown the new standard of African governance was far from universal. "ALMA is critical, and we're putting a lot of faith in it, but it also makes me nervous," said Basu. "I worry about those countries that still look at malaria programs as a handout, because the moment you go away, those programs will fall apart. And Africa's record of making each other accountable is spotty. But I have no other answer to the sustainability question. I can't think of any alternative. It's the only way forward."

CHAPTER 14

Countless

The final year of the campaign—2010—should have been great. Africa was being covered by what was, in effect, one vast bed net. The malaria map was shrinking. In the past few years, malaria had been halved in ten African countries: Botswana, Cape Verde, Eritrea, Madagascar, Namibia, Rwanda, São Tomé and Príncipe, South Africa, Swaziland, and Zambia.[1] Outside Africa, thirty-two out of fifty-six countries had done the same. Morocco, the United Arab Emirates, and Turkmenistan declared they were malaria free. Zanzibar announced it had all but eliminated the disease for the third time.[2] Hundreds of thousands of Africans were no longer dying. Millions were not getting sick. Billions of dollars were being better spent. After millennia of suffering and death, humankind was finally overcoming Original Disease.

The success of the campaign reflected well on Chambers's methods. He made aid an integral concern of business and, in Nigeria, religion, and a priority for Western government and

African governments. He achieved that not just by playing on good intentions but by relying on self-interest, something that also answered the perennial aid question of sustainability. Chambers had made aid efficient and results-oriented by importing business tools. One of those—his specialty, leverage—had allowed him to create one of the largest campaigns the world had ever seen.

The campaign also confirmed Jeffrey Sachs was right: health and prosperity were linked and the key to Africa's upward trajectory. Five of the ten African countries that had halved malaria—Botswana, Cape Verde, Namibia, South Africa, and Swaziland—were among Africa's eight middle-income countries. (The other three are Mauritius, the Seychelles, and Lesotho, all of which are already malaria free.) Four of the five other countries were also among those whose GDP was growing the fastest: Madagascar grew an average annual 5.7 percent from 2004 to 2008, Rwanda an average 8.6 percent, São Tomé and Príncipe 6.1 percent, and Zambia 5.8 percent. (The exception was Eritrea, where an autocratic ruler was able to dictate action on malaria, even while his country shrank under diplomatic and economic isolation for its support of Islamist rebels in Somalia.) If the World Malaria Report had included statistics from 2010, it would have found Ethiopia had also halved malaria by the middle of that year, all the while managing average annual economic growth of 11.8 percent from 2004 to 2008.[3]

There was still a problem with Africans relying on others to fix their problems. But ALMA was one answer to that, with the potential to transform how all assistance was delivered. And after all the scandal and controversy that surrounded aid, Chambers's results promised reinvention and deliverance. He had achieved his success working with the big aid institutions that were so often the target of criticism. They could now replicate their success in other campaigns. Tony Blair, whose Faith Foundation was assisting the Muslim-Christian collaboration in Nigeria, told me the malaria campaign was "about as good an example as you get" of how "the nature of help is changing" and how that, in turn, was "rebalancing the respectability of the aid case."[4]

Proof of that came in how the aid world was increasingly adopting Chambers's ideas. At the WHO, Margaret Chan said he helped inspire her to reform her own organization. "I come from Hong Kong," she said. "Very entrepreneurial. Anything goes. Businesses serve people well, and they move with the times. But the WHO was born sixty years ago. When I first joined, I kept asking myself: is it still relevant? Clearly, it should be able to move faster." Watching Chambers, she said, "it dawned on me. *I* should leverage *Ray*. I should use his network and his ability to use good business sense at the WHO." Writing a malaria business plan for the WHO, with targets and deadlines, had set a particularly useful precedent. "Eradicating malaria is an ambitious goal, a dream even. But if we hadn't demanded that, scientists and aid professionals would never have gone back to the drawing board. We would just have continued as before."[5]

Likewise the British and US governments, the two biggest funders in malaria and all aid, are also following Chambers's example. In January 2011, Rajiv Shah, head of the American agency USAID, announced that Washington wanted to see a transformation of aid into something more "businesslike." USAID conducted nearly five hundred independent evaluations of its work in 1990, said Shah. That fell to a hundred seventy in 2008, despite a threefold increase in programs. Often the evaluations were commissioned by the aid project itself—"a relationship between implementing partners and evaluators akin to that between investment banks and ratings agencies"—and followed "a two-two-two model." "Two contractors spending two weeks abroad conducting two dozen interviews. For about $30,000, they produce a report that no one needs and no one reads. And the results they claim often have little grounding in fact. One of our implementing partners . . . claimed over a quarter of a million people benefited from a $14,000 rehabilitation of an Iraqi morgue." USAID needed to move beyond "updat[ing] the traditional version of an aid agency. Instead, we are seeking to build something greater: a modern development enterprise."[6]

The next month, the British International Development Secretary, Andrew Mitchell, announced that London would also "focus ruthlessly on results," cutting £50 million of funding to aid agencies it considered poor performers and boosting support to star performers. In Ethiopia his department was setting up the first ever "cash on delivery" aid project, a scheme to enroll girls in school in which funding would be released only when results were achieved. "From now on we will only give aid where we can follow the money and ensure that the British taxpayer is getting value for money," said Mitchell. "Most international organisations are doing a decent job but some need to be shown the yellow card. Others will, frankly, get the bullet."[7]

The implications beyond aid were no less profound. The campaign had given religion a new pragmatic purpose on which it might base a revival, something understood by the Methodists in the US, who pledged to raise $75 million for the Global Fund.[8] In Nigeria, it had given Christianity and Islam a cause around which they could unite and overcome their bloody rivalry.

What worked for God worked for Mammon too. Victoria Beckham suddenly had a point. And if aid was becoming more businesslike, business was becoming more aidlike. In the winner-takes-all boom that began in the 1980s, the winners had ended up taking an awful lot. Chambers amassed hundreds of millions of dollars. Bill Gates and the financier Warren Buffett accrued fortunes several times larger than those of entire nations. Chambers had been one of the first to make the switch from narrow personal gain to enlightened self-interest in his own life. His campaign was pointing the way forward to a new, inclusive way of business. In particular, he and his team had cast a giant bed net around the world, a statement of inclusion without parallel.

Malaria was opening the doors to a gentler, more inclusive world. Business now had a way out of the resource curse. Fighting malaria was proof that helping others less fortunate ultimately helped everyone. Yawning inequality wasn't just bad taste but bad business. Unfair was one thing. Unwise was something else.

Those ideas are becoming ever more common in business. Profits remain a priority, but many CEOs now view them as something unlikely to be maximized in isolation. The lone buccaneer is out. In are companies that see their future prosperity as best guaranteed by membership of a prosperous, healthy society. The new mantra is "doing well by doing good." Fashion giants such as Nike now take notice of conditions in the Asian factories where their sneakers are made. Organic certification has moved from niche to mainstream supermarket fare. McKinsey, the consultancy, now has a division researching poor-world development. De Beers forswears blood diamonds. Discussions at the elite business forum the World Economic Forum in Davos, once dominated by talk of personal profits and narrow opportunity, now take a wider view of return on investment, one that encompasses development and poverty alleviation. Talk at the Forum's January 2011 meeting was even dominated by the issue of inequality and its corrective, inclusion. The fury that Western bankers and their bonuses attract is best understood in this context. It's not just the amounts of money involved. It's the ethos of exclusivity—personal reward defined solely in returns to the individual—that is increasingly out of step with the times.

Likewise, we are now in a new age of philanthropy. Some call it philanthro-capitalism. Bill Gates calls it creative capitalism. Whatever name you use, it is dramatic. Rather than drip-dripping donations away in perpetuity as earlier foundations tended to do, the new philanthropists aim to give away most of their money in their own lifetimes and all of it within a few decades. This high-impact approach is measured in some extraordinary figures. According to one study, overall private donations in the US hit a new record of $306 billion in 2007—around a third of the value of all car sales in the US that year.[9] In 2008, the Index for Global Philanthropy found total private US foreign aid was $37.3 billion, $10 billion more than the US government sent overseas.[10] The trend has been most marked among the richest of the rich. In 2006, twenty-one Americans donated at least $100 million each to charitable causes, nearly double the number that did so in 2005. A fresh high came on August 4, 2010, when Gates and Buffett persuaded forty of the world's richest—among them Oracle founder Larry Ellison, Citigroup creator Sandy Weill, Star Wars director George Lucas, media mogul Barry Diller, and eBay founder Peter Omidyar—to announce they would all be giving away at least half their fortunes, much of it to the developing world.

The new mood also extends beyond business. With its central argument that we—different races, different animals, even different insects and plants—are all part of the same world, the environmental movement is a standout example of the new inclusion. So is the technological tool of the age, the internet, which was founded on collaboration and freedom, and whose most popular products and services are often free.

Politics too is changing. A generation after Margaret Thatcher told Britain there was "no such thing as society," her successor as Conservative Party prime minister, David Cameron, promised to inaugurate the "Big Society," a nation that had volunteerism, local democracy, and collective social responsibility at its core. French president Nicholas Sarkozy proposes ending measuring a country's wealth in the narrow count of euros denoted by Gross Domestic Product and using something more ephemeral: Gross National Happiness. In China, the annual session of the National People's Congress in March 2011 declared that a "happy China" was more important than a rich one and enshrined that as the goal of its new five-year plan. In the US, critics accuse President Barack Obama of extending socialism with his health care reforms. In reality his policies are not communist but communitarian, based on the belief that a country's cohesion is key to its welfare and prosperity and something for a government to encourage with national infrastructure like roads, waterworks, power, and, yes, a minimum standard of health care.

Chambers performed his own transformation as long ago as 1985. He was one of those who launched the get-rich-quick era. Within a few years, he was leading attempts to rectify the inequality he helped create, arguing it was ultimately in his own interest. At first, he was simply figuring out a new way to be in the world. Today it can seem as if he was sketching out a new way for the world to be.

And yet the climax of the campaign that defined the new inclusion—the December 31, 2010, deadline for universal malaria bed-net coverage—passed largely unnoticed. There were reasons for that. Chambers and his team ended the year on a sour note when he had to make an emergency visit to Zambia. The country had cut malaria deaths by 66 percent by 2009. But allegations of corruption in the health ministry had surfaced, and in June 2010 the Global Fund froze $300 million in grants. As in Kenya, that meant millions of expiring nets would not be replaced. Crisis loomed. Once again, Chambers secured alternative funding of $30 million from the World Bank, but not before malaria rates began to climb.

The Zambian allegations, however, turned out to be the harbinger of something even worse. In January 2011, the inevitable finally happened: malaria got busted. As well as the $3.5 million in undocumented spending and $7 million on "unsupported and ineligible costs" at the Zambian health ministry, the Associated Press revealed an internal Global Fund investigation had found:

- $4.1 million—67 percent—of money spent on an anti-AIDS program in Mauritania disappeared in "pervasive fraud."
- $4 million of $22.6 million spent on a malaria and tuberculosis program in Mali was stolen using "rampant" forgery.
- 30 percent of grants to Djibouti were misused to buy cars and motorcycles, while $750,000 simply disappeared.

Accusatory headlines alleging fraud in the world's biggest aid campaign—"Gates's and Bono's favorite," said many—appeared in almost every newspaper and on every website in the world. The Fund announced a panel of experts to examine the Fund's ability to fight fraud and plans to raise its inspector-general's resources from $3 million and two assistants to $19 million and thirty assistants. Bill Gates tried to defend the Fund, noting that the missing money concerned less than a third of 1 percent of the Fund's grants and the Fund had uncovered the fraud itself. But, as he added in an interview with the Associated Press, the adverse publicity might mean "people will reduce their generosity—and that causes deaths." He was right, at least about the first part. Sweden suspended its annual donation of $85 million. Germany put a stop on its pledge of $250 million.[11]

Meanwhile, throughout 2010 Chambers had also been forced to confront his own uncomfortable reality: he was going to miss his target. Originally, he'd set himself the goal of distributing 300 million nets to 600 million people by December 31, 2010. And he did that, or very nearly. By year's end, 289 million nets had gone out to 578 million people—an astonishing 300,000 nets delivered every day for thirty-two months.[12] What's more, surveys showed that 80 percent of the nets were being used.[13]

But the goalposts had shifted. Estimates of the numbers he needed to cover had risen during the campaign, first from 600 million people to 700 million, then to 765 million. That meant Chambers had to hand out another eighty-three million nets at a cost of a further $830 million—and he spent much of the year in negotiations with net manufacturers. In the end, he found both the nets and the funding, but not in time to meet the deadline. Distribution was complete in South Sudan and Ethiopia. It was unfinished in Kenya, Nigeria, Tanzania, the DRC, and Uganda—where the government was still adamant about buying only African nets, even if they were slower to arrive.

Again, Chambers didn't miss by much. The nets were paid for, ordered, or in place in all those places. Kenya, Uganda, and Nigeria were expected to have completed their distributions in the first half of 2011, which would bring net coverage up to 90 percent. The DRC, the eternal laggard, was not expected to do the same until September or October. But even that failure contained a valuable lesson: the DRC was doable. "Five years ago, no one would touch this country with a barge pole," said Basu. "People would simply concentrate on working with the blue-eyed boys of development, like Tanzania. Enough international goodwill to fully fund every net that the DRC needs was unheard of. But Ray managed to get traction behind the DRC in a way that made it impossible to ignore any longer."[14] Alan Court said both South Sudan and the DRC had proved "counterintuitive." "There is a huge desire to have these nets," he said. "The people know about nets, they know how to use them, and they want them."[15] In an environment of desperate need, all it took to make an enormous change was a few people with the right resources. "When the history of malaria is written," commented Steven Phillips, "it's going to be one about a few key leaders."[16]

Universal coverage would still be achieved, just later than hoped. Yet when I spoke to Chambers at his home in Morristown, New Jersey, on December 28, three days before the deadline expired, he was subdued. "Every day we delay, we are losing hundreds, perhaps thousands, of children," he said. "The house is on fire until we get everybody under a net. It's very frustrating. We could have reached full coverage by the end of the year. We did not, because of inexcusable delays. I hate the thought of losing those children."

The sense of deflation was increased by the realization that 2010 was not the end. Over that last year, Chambers and his staff had struggled with the gnawing suspicion that their deadline was artificial. In reality, there was no finishing line with malaria—at least not for decades. Whether ALMA took over or whether Chambers and his team remained in place, the campaign had to go on. "When we began to think about replacement nets—that all the nets we'd handed out would be expiring after three years and sprays would have to be repeated annually—that was really difficult to get our heads around," said Basu. "It meant there was no actual state of universal coverage. The nets constantly expire. There is no moment you can stand still. This was a remarkably ambitious and hugely successful public initiative. But we had to go through three or four more cycles of nets and spraying at least before there was a decent hope of eliminating malaria, and more like six or seven in the worst places. It was like we'd been climbing this mountain for so long and when we finally get to the summit, we see four more peaks ahead of us. It's not what you expect. You expect to be elated, maybe raise a glass of champagne. And it was: 'Shit! We're exhausted! And there's another four mountains!'"

The team left their offices for Christmas in a mood of anticlimax. "I was sitting in the office on December 23," says Basu. "We have these little countdown clocks on all our desks, and I was looking at them and talking to Tim. And I said, 'There is going to be no great moment, you know? This is not a bang. It's a whimper.' The feeling was just one of exhaustion. We'd had this mad focus for more than two and a half years, the last few months had been really tiring, and then Zambia was just a tough way to end the year."

A few of the campaigners were celebrating. A year before the deadline, Chambers's Malaria No More cofounder Peter Chernin had warned against expecting 100 percent. "Perfection is the enemy of good," he said. "Will we cover every single person with a bed net? Honestly, I doubt it. Will we have a bigger impact than any other campaign ever? Yes, I think we will. You set lofty goals, and if you get 90 percent, that's a great achievement, and you focus on getting the remaining 10 percent done as quickly as you can."[17] Others could barely contain their glee. "It's unbelievable," said Tachi Yamada at the Gates Foundation in December 2010. "It's amazing. In parts of Africa, malaria is absolutely going away. It's testament to what the world can do if it really wants to."[18] Christian Lengeler of the Swiss Tropical Institute was little short of ecstatic. "It's a wonderful feeling, I tell you, to be able to contribute to this," he said. "It's great! Malaria was so big, it was felt there was nothing we could do about it. People said we were not going to change anything. It's such an extraordinary story."[19]

But celebration was still something that did not come naturally to much of the aid world. One reason why the malaria campaign had grown so large, appearing on prime time television and at the top of the Western agenda, was Chambers's presentation of its subject as approachable, even entertaining. But the rest of the aid world was still finding it hard to give up the old ways of "raising awareness": intimidating the public with dire warnings of imminent crisis. When, in the teeth of a recession and government debt crisis in October 2010, Western donors still pledged $11.5 billion to the Global Fund for 2011–2013, up from $9.7 billion in 2007, the aid world reacted with outrage and moral blackmail. "The outcome of this conference is absolutely key for millions of people around the world, and this will not take us to where we were hoping to be," said Michel Kazatchkine, the Global Fund's executive director, explaining that the target had been $13 billion. Médecins Sans Frontières declared the decision to "massively underfund" the Global Fund "will cost lives and severely weaken the ability of countries to implement programs" to beat back disease. Asia Russell of Health GAP, a US HIV/AIDS and human rights activist group, called the donor announcement "a flop."[20]

Likewise, in October 2010 Greenwood's former student Bob Snow published a report warning that although annual international funding for malaria had increased since 2007 by 166 percent, from $730 million to $1.94 billion, this was still 60 percent short of what was needed. Only twenty-one out of ninety-three countries had enough money to implement effective control measures, wrote Snow in the *Lancet*. "Any decline in malaria-funding commitments will run the risk of a resurgence of malaria," he added. "A failure to maintain the momentum will mean money spent so far will have been for nothing."[21] Snow was correct to argue that the campaign had to be maintained. The WHO's failure to sustain its earlier efforts had been a disaster. As Richard Feachem, former executive director of the Global Fund, said, with malaria "success is the enemy of sustainability, because if you blink, it will come back with a vengeance."[22]

But the malaria world's lack of acknowledgment of its own achievements was striking nonetheless and hinted at the same motivations that persuaded other aid workers not to solve crises but merely manage them. Success wasn't something the malaria world wanted to hear. Its interests demanded continued catastrophe, even when that flew in the face of reality.

An inability to rejoice could not explain away the criticism the campaign was attracting, however. Some of that came from within. Marcel Tanner predicted that if *Plasmodium falciparum* was beaten back, *Plasmodium vivax*, long a far lesser threat, would surge in its place. "It's crap to talk about elimination without talking about *vivax*," he said. "If we reduce *falciparum*, a good indication that we have been successful will be that *vivax* comes up."[23]

Outside the campaign, others argued the goal of eradication was too far-fetched, and perhaps even counterproductive. Critics said a more modest one—control—would be more effective. In October 2010 Sonia Shah, the malaria historian, wrote a front-page essay in the esteemed French international affairs newspaper *Le Monde Diplomatique* with the headline "Live with It." She argued that new evidence indicating malaria was passed to humans from gorillas and monkeys meant malaria might be impossible to eradicate. "What if there's a secret reservoir of pathogens in the bodies of wild animals, unreachable by medical interventions, as there is in yellow fever, cholera, and influenza, diseases from which humankind can never hope to be completely free?" In those circumstances, controlling the disease was the only sensible goal. "When public health leaders want to control a disease, they devote the majority of their resources to the areas of greatest need. When their goal is eradication, then they must spend their resources on areas where eradication is most likely—the areas with the least need. If malaria eradication campaigns fail, their resources and political capital will have been lavished on the lowest priority areas with the lightest burdens of disease."[24]

The same month, the *Lancet* published a series of articles on malaria that echoed those criticisms. Eradication, while a noble goal, "could lead to dangerous swings in funding and political commitment," read the magazine's editorial. It accused Margaret Chan's World Health Organization of failing "to rise to their responsibilities to give the malaria community essential direction. The quest for elimination must not distract existing good malaria control work."[25]

The critics made a good theoretical point: fighting malaria in places where other diseases were a bigger problem would be a waste of money, and elimination of malaria was not feasible in the worst places in the short term. But some of the critiques ignored the reality that Chambers and his team weren't targeting countries peripheral to malaria in the hope of knocking off some easy targets for eradication. They were focusing on the core. Nor were control and eradication two different things. The first was a stepping-stone to the second—which, as both sides pointed out, was anyway several decades distant and unlikely without an effective vaccine.

Other critics were guilty of displaying another old aid world weakness: burying themselves in academic debate while a changing reality superseded them on the ground. As the malaria campaign progressed in 2009 and 2010, development specialists found themselves distracted by a technical dispute over the merits of "vertical interventions"—single-focus projects, such as a project to build a well or a campaign to fix malaria—and "horizontal inventions"—broader programs to improve, say, an African government's ability to deliver clean water or its national health system. The malaria campaign was actually both: it targeted a specific disease and also built up capacity and health services in the course of doing so. "We can use these systems, and the things we have learned, on multiple diseases," said Chernin. "We are learning how to get the message delivered, how to use celebrities and faith leaders and football stars, and that has implications far beyond malaria." That didn't stop the theorists from doing battle, or even dismissing the malaria campaign for its supposed vertical focus. Comments about the malaria campaign from Professor Ian Linden, director of the Faiths Act Programme at the Tony Blair Faith Foundation, were typical: "I think there is a serious issue that the massive vertical intervention is not necessarily going to be positive for building up health systems," he said. "It's not necessarily sustainable. When you drive off into the sunset, the community is left behind."[26]

It was a similar story in the Grand Aid Debate. By combining business and aid, Chambers had carved a middle path between the pro-aid evangelists such as Jeffrey Sachs and aid critics such as William Easterly and Dambisa Moyo. "On malaria, we have an example where aid is working," said Basu, "because it's being done in a different way from the way traditional development has been done. You see it in the results and the efficiency."

But Sachs and Easterly carried on sparring regardless. On May 24, 2009, Sachs posted a furious essay in the online *Huffington Post* headlined "Aid Ironies." Sachs did cite the malaria campaign in his post and elaborated on its achievements in a follow-up. But the thrust of his article was a personal attack on Easterly and Moyo. "The debate about foreign aid has become farcical," he wrote.

> The big opponents of aid today are Dambisa Moyo, an African-born economist who reportedly received scholarships so that she could go to Harvard and Oxford but sees nothing wrong with denying $10 in aid to an African child for an anti-malaria bed net. Her colleague in opposing aid, Bill Easterly, received large-scale government support from the National Science Foundation for his own graduate training. I certainly don't begrudge any of them the help that they got. Far from it. I believe in this kind of help. And I'd find Moyo's views cruel and mistaken even if she did not get the scholarships that have been reported. I begrudge them trying to pull up the ladder for those still left behind. Before peddling their simplistic concoction of free markets and self-help, they and we should think about the realities of life, in which all of us need help at some time or other and in countless ways, and even more importantly we should think about the life-and-death consequences for impoverished people who are denied that help. . . . Rich people have an uncanny ability to oppose aid for everybody but themselves.[27]

Easterly responded the next day under the headline "Sachs Ironies: Why Critics Are Better for Foreign Aid Than Apologists." He wrote, "Official foreign aid agencies delivering aid to Africa are used to operating with nobody holding them accountable for aid dollars actually reaching poor people. Now that establishment is running scared with the emergence of independent African voices critical of aid, such as that of Dambisa Moyo. Jeffrey Sachs, the world's leading apologist and fund-raiser for the aid establishment, has responded here with a ferocious personal attack on Moyo and myself." Easterly stressed he didn't oppose all aid, just bad aid, and that Sachs knew that, not least because Sachs had quoted Easterly in his work. "Sachs suffers from the same acute shortage of truthiness as did the Bush/Cheney administration. . . . Any aid critic is immediately denounced as a heartless baby-killer, which protects the establishment from the accountability so badly needed to see aid reach the poor."[28]

The following day Moyo weighed in, writing that Sachs's personal attack was "just the latest example of using this tactic to obfuscate the facts and avoid addressing the fundamental issues regarding aid's manifest failure to deliver on its promise of generating growth and alleviating poverty in Africa. . . . There is no country—anywhere in the world—that has meaningfully reduced poverty and spurred significant and sustainable levels of economic growth by relying on aid. Mr. Sachs knows this; how do I know? He taught me while I was studying at Harvard."[29]

Sachs could not let that lie. "Ms. Dambisa Moyo's recent *Huffington Post* article exposes the confusions that underlie her slashing attacks on aid," he wrote the next day. "Moyo is not offering a reasoned or evidence-based position on aid. Moyo wants to cut aid off dramatically, even if that leaves millions to die."[30]

If all that wasn't enough to overshadow the malaria campaign, the big malaria stories of 2010 and early 2011 were about

celebrities who had contracted the disease: British tabloid favorite
Cheryl Cole, the Ivorian and Chelsea soccer player Didier Drogba,
and George Clooney. Between a corruption scandal, the noise of
clashing aid heavyweights, and the drama of sickly superstars, one
of the most successful aid campaigns of all time was forgotten.

It might have been different if the campaigners could say how
many lives they had saved. In business, profits are tracked by the
week and reports issued on a quarterly basis. Aid doesn't announce
its results in the same regularized fashion. That's partly because aid
is slow—in malaria's case, somewhat unavoidably, since gathering
data from tens of thousands of villages is a long process—and
partly because aid agencies have no common measurements.

But mostly it is because malaria is very difficult to measure.
Lengeler said that because malaria often went undiagnosed and
since most malaria deaths happened outside a hospital and were
not reported, it was all but impossible to measure quickly and
accurately how many people died from the disease. The total
number of child deaths in a country could be estimated by taking
a sample and multiplying it, and a number for malaria deaths ex-
trapolated from that. But even those statistics took two to three
years to come in. Moreover, they generally measured average
child mortality rates over the past five years, figures that would
underplay the effect of a dramatic, all-out attack on malaria.

That meant the *World Malaria Report 2010* was actually a
misnomer. Its conclusions and assessments were based on data
from 2009 or before. Chambers wouldn't know how many lives
he had saved for another year or more. The belief was that millions of children were walking around who otherwise wouldn't
have been. But the only thing anyone knew for sure was that
Chambers had missed his targets.

But surely it was possible to work out a rough idea of the results? I asked Lengeler to help me make two estimates: lives saved and at what cost. Taking the second part first, figuring out the cost was relatively easy. The Roll Back Malaria report of 2010 estimated 42 million nets distributed to Nigeria would save 121,000 children's lives. That meant every 347.1 nets saved one child's life. Lengeler's own estimate was more like every 180 nets. Either way, if every net cost $10, that was somewhere between $1,800 and $3,500 for every child's life. That was a lot more than "$10 buys a net, saves a child's life," as Chambers had it in his catchphrase. But $3,500 is still pretty cheap for a life. It also compared well with Easterly's figure of $3,521 to raise a poor person's income by $3.65 a year, not least because over a lifetime, even in the poorest countries in the world, every saved child could be expected to earn considerably more than $3,500. This was further proof of the proposition that by helping others you helped yourself. Fighting malaria didn't just save lives. It saved money too.

But the big question was: How many children had Chambers saved? The *2009 World Malaria Report* reported that malaria cases around the world were fairly constant from 2005 to 2008, falling slightly from 244 million to 243 million. After Chambers began his campaign, they plunged. By 2009, the number of malaria cases was 225 million. The fall in deaths was more impressive: from 863,000 in 2008 to 781,000 in 2009—82,000 lives saved in a single year.[31]

Chambers had delivered twice as many nets in 2010 as 2009. So the numbers of lives he saved should also have roughly doubled, to a ballpark hundred fifty thousand. That made a total of around a quarter of a million lives saved during the thirty-two months of the campaign.[32]

That rough estimate was backed up by Roll Back Malaria's 2010 report, released in September of that year. It estimated that by 2010 around 175,000 lives were now being saved every year because of the campaign, although it added a wide margin of error: the figure could be as low as 120,000 or as high as 250,000. Plus, because it had used a far lower figure for coverage in Nigeria than was now the case, the real figure for lives saved per year by the end of 2010 was probably 121,000 more—making a median figure of 300,000.[33]

Roll Back Malaria made predictions for the years ahead too. If universal coverage had been achieved by the end of 2010 and was maintained through replacement of worn-out nets for the next five years, then the number of lives saved by the end of 2015 would be 2.95 million. If universal coverage were only achieved by 2015, that figure would still be 2.15 million. In an excited email in June 2011, Basu told me Kenya was done—"Truly amazing turnaround, Mugo delivered, her and Ray now have a close friendship, we really need her." He added that Tanzania, Nigeria, Uganda (now without a sacked Minister Mallinga) and even the DRC should all join in between August and October. By finishing in 2011, Chambers could be expected to be somewhere between 2.15 and 2.95 million lives saved. Lengeler said that felt about right. "Whether it's 2 million or 2.5 million or 2.7 million, it's still a lot," he said. "It's millions. There's no doubt about that."[34]

I realized the sheer number of people saved—millions—was actually hindering attempts to count them. Measuring malaria deaths was all but impossible. Now that so many were being avoided, any effort to add them up was also hopeless. The number of people saved was literally countless. You couldn't quantify it with any precision. But maybe you could feel it.

CHAPTER 15

Fine and Fair

My taxi driver, David, is late picking me up from Entebbe airport, and we hit the evening rush hour in Kampala, so it's 10 PM before we cross the Nile and start on the road to Apac. Twenty-one days before the end of 2010, after all the lofty talk and frantic campaigning, I want to see whether the fight against malaria is working in the place it faces its stiffest challenge. But as David edges off the tarmac and onto the rutted mud tracks to Apac, I begin to worry. The *funestus* feeds at night. Crossing Kwania's swamps, we have to keep the windows down to stop the windshield steaming up. The last time I visited Apac I drove myself, but this time David has insisted on making up for his lateness by taking the wheel—and while I did warn him about malaria, his manner suggests he thinks I am exaggerating. And I have doubts the campaign has reached Apac. It is remote, and Uganda has been one of Chambers's biggest headaches. As we drive deeper into the swamps, David tells me he's just returned from three years in Iraq working as a security guard. He should be home with his wife and son, Newton. Instead I'm taking him to the global epicenter of our oldest and deadliest disease.

About three miles outside Apac, we see light ahead. We're upon it, then past it, in a flash. I struggle to process what I've just seen: a large open fire in front of a roadside beer stall and perhaps forty people dancing, singing, and drinking. Soon we see another light. This one belongs to a restaurant, with plastic seats and a small fence. There's more music, and here perhaps a hundred people are dancing and chatting. David mutters something about crazy country folk. *Crazy is right*, I think. *They're out in the open.*

As we roll into Apac, I can see that, despite the hour, the streets are packed. People are walking, cycling, chatting with their neighbors, sitting in a number of open-air bars. I direct David to the Lamco B. It's full. We try another place, the Tani Guesthouse. It's also booked up. The receptionist directs us to a bungalow on the outskirts of town that is hiring out rooms for $10 a night. I am shown to a clean-looking bedroom containing a double bed and a bed net. I scan the walls for mosquitoes and am mildly surprised to find none. I cover myself in repellent, take my Malarone pill, dress in long trousers, long-sleeve shirt, and socks and climb under the net.

The next morning, December 11, we drive to the Apac district hospital. Sixteen months before, the streets had been deserted except for three naked men. Now we find ourselves forced to slow to walking pace as we push through crowds of hundreds. There are scores of young women dressed in blue and white uniforms—trainee nurses, I discover later. Where shops had been shuttered before, now mechanics are banging wheel frames, metal workers are soldering iron gates, timber merchants are unloading wood, and soda stores are unloading the latest delivery from trucks. Several places have a fresh coat of paint. One of them is the Sunset Lodge, which now also boasts a packed café in front. I realize I haven't seen a single mosquito. I check myself for bites. Nothing.

At the hospital I find Martin, finishing up his night shift on the children's ward. I ask to see the admissions book. There are three children recorded as being admitted with malaria the day before. There are none the day before that, then two, then one. Most of the admissions are not for malaria but pneumonia, tuberculosis, and burns. I walk onto the ward. The smell has gone. There are bed nets on every bed. I start to count the number of patients, but as I do, I feel my throat tighten and my eyes blur, and I have to step outside. Only ten of the thirty-six beds are being used.

"Martin," I say when I have composed myself, "things have changed."

Martin smiles. "We used to have fifteen patients a day with malaria," he says. "Now it is fifteen a week. The ward was completely full. Now, you see there is a lot of improvement. A lot."

"Where have all the mosquitoes gone?" I ask.

"Actually, that is the difference," he says. "There used to be a lot of mosquitoes in Apac. Too many. When you were sitting outside, you had them crawling all over you. But then we got the nets, and they did some spraying, and it cleared them." He searches for the right words, then gestures to the blue sky. "Now it is fair here," he declares. "Apac is fine and fair."

We drive to the Lamco B to find my old landlord, Lameck. The receptionist tells me he is out at his village home three miles away and gives us directions. We arrive to find Lameck overseeing a team of builders putting a second story on what will soon be Lamco C. He bounds out of the site to greet us and takes us on a tour of his new place. To one side, Lameck has planted a copse of young fir trees, a forest of mangoes and bananas, and a field of tomatoes. At the back are pens—Lameck is diversifying into chickens and goats too. Inside the new building, Lameck explains Lamco C will have ten en suite rooms, all set around an open courtyard. Lameck has built two open-air sitting areas where his guests can enjoy the evening air. He anticipates my question.

"Oh, there's less malaria," he beams at me. "There's less mosquitoes. There's no problem being outside now." Then, gesturing at the new open-air lounges, "It'll be nice, no?"

It's amazing, I say.

We drive to the District Health Office, where I find Dr. Matthew Emer still at his desk. His office has changed. It's somehow brighter, sunnier. Looking around, I realize there are no longer any screens on the windows. The fan is off. Dr. Emer smiles and says he has "a lot of news."

In 2010, the district health authority finally won its case against the organic farmers and was allowed to restart spraying insecticide. Worried that their previous partial coverage of Apac could have produced a DDT-resistant mosquito, Dr. Emer's staff did tests—and sure enough, DDT was no longer effective. A second insecticide had little effect as well. Then in August they tried a third insecticide, Bendiocarb. That worked. And in September and October, a long promised delivery of a hundred sixty-eight thousand bed nets arrived, the first tranche in Uganda's two-step Global Fund delivery, intended for children under five and pregnant women.

The combined effect of the spraying and the nets, says Dr. Emer, "was fantastic. By the end of the month, we had village after village completely free from mosquitoes. Everybody noticed. The feedback was overwhelming. There was a massive decline in malaria." He shows me his new figures. Until August, the statistics describe a situation unchanged: as low as 1,550 cases in the first week of 2010, as high as 4,966 in the third week of June, and a rough average of 3,000 to 3,500 a week. But after the spraying began, there was a sudden drop. In the second week of the month, Apac recorded 3,594 cases of malaria. The following week that was down to 2,843, then 2,426, then 2,120. After the nets began arriving, it plunged even more, to 1,684, then 1,385, and 1,269 in the last week of September. For October and November it rose a little before settling at around 1,800 cases a month. In a few weeks, malaria had been halved. "We have high hopes," he says. "We think we're very likely to be able to engineer a reversal."

Success has encouraged him to set up an additional range of antimalaria programs. Pregnant women are now receiving presumptive malaria treatment: automatic doses of antimalaria medicine to protect their unborn babies. His staff is fanning out to all the tin-roofed, wood-shack dispensaries in the area, showing pharmacists how to use new rapid diagnostic tests—small blood examination kits that can prove or disprove malaria within fifteen minutes—and to keep records of what they find. They are also training thousands of village health workers, one for every twenty to thirty people, in malaria diagnosis and bednet use.

There are still problems, of course. Dr. Emer says he doesn't yet have the staff he needs. Only one doctor applied to work in Apac and, when he got the job, never showed up. The government in Kampala is also cutting back. And Dr. Emer says it looks as though Apac will miss Chambers's universal bed-net coverage target by a few weeks. He does not expect a second set of nets until after the new year.

Still, Dr. Emer's complaints feel perfunctory. He doesn't look unhappy. Apac feels reborn, I venture. It's as though I have pressed a detonator. "You can see it!" he exclaims, gesturing wildly at the window. "You can witness it! Less children sick! Parents spending less money on medicine! Mothers spending more time on their gardens and going to the markets rather than spending four to five days every few months in hospital!"

Apac isn't the only thing that's changed, I add.

"I am changed," he acknowledges. "I am happy. I am really, really happy. When you went to the hospital before, it was full, full of people wailing and dying. You saw it for yourself! You couldn't count them! Now our interventions are working. You can see, for the first time ever, that we are going to get on top of malaria. We're really doing it! There is a reason to smile here again."

David and I have one more stop before we leave Apac. We drive back to the hospital, and I walk over to the registrar's office, where I ask Julius, the statistician, to show me some more numbers. Julius has a record of every outpatient for the last three years up to September 2010 and for every inpatient for the three years up to October 2010.

Among outpatients, I see that when I visited before, September 2009, there were 1,210 children under five treated in the hospital for malaria. A year later that number has come down to 647. The figures are more dramatic for inpatients: in September 2009, 235 children were admitted for malaria. By September

2010, that has come down to 121, and in October it falls further, to 94.

I look at the column headed "Mortality." In the past, I can see the hospital would lose an average of ten to fifteen children a month. September 2009 was better than average: just three boys and one girl. But by September 2010, there's been a substantial improvement on even that figure: just one girl died. And then, on the next line, I see it. In the month of October 2010, in the only hospital in the most malarious town on earth, no child dies of malaria.

Acknowledgments

This book would have been impossible without the support of my editors at *Time*, in particular Michael Elliott, Rick Stengel, and John Huey, who backed my interest in malaria from the start and paid for far more trips across Africa to research the subject than was strictly necessary for a cover story. *Time* is one of the last news outlets in the world where it's still possible to spend months or years reporting a single story. As a developing-world correspondent pursuing what are often unobvious stories, I am only too aware that the encouragement and freedom I enjoy likely border on financially unwise. Gentlemen, as ever, I am in your debt.

This book also owes its existence to Michael Dwyer at Hurst, who rescued it when no one else would have it. Michael, thank you for being such a source of encouragement and for taking on such an unlikely sounding subject. Thanks also to Terry Morris, Andrea Nattrass, Wesley Thompson, and all at Macmillan SA, the greatest publishing team in South Africa, with whom I continue to enjoy a fantastic relationship. In the United States Susan Weinberg and Clara Platter, my editor at PublicAffairs, moved with a speed that broke several records in the publishing world, all the more remarkable for the fact that the manuscript landed on Clara's desk on her first day on the job. My deep thanks to them, and to Lindsay Fradkoff, Jaime Leifer, Pete Garceau, and Sandra Beris, and to Beth Wright at Trio Bookworks.

The story of how Ray Chambers and his team saved millions of lives is not well-known. The only reason I can tell it here is because of the unprecedented access offered to me by Ray and his staff. Not only did they allow me to travel with them across Africa on a number of occasions, but they also agreed to an almost never-ending set of interviews without a word of complaint. Ray, and Protik, Alan, Tim, Sean, Jamie: I only hope I have justified your faith.

The enthusiasm and helpfulness I received from the UN special envoy's office were replicated across the malaria world. Over the two years I spent reporting on the subject, I spoke to countless individuals with far more important things to do than answer my queries and correct my ignorance. Of particular help were Steven Phillips, who helped me understand how big a story this was on a sickening car ride across Rwanda (thanks too to Steven's wife, Isabel, who provided advice on structure and narrative); Christian Lengeler, who steered me through the science and whose enthusiasm for the cause infected me every time I spoke to him; Steve Knowles, who not only opened my eyes in Ghana but also nursed me when something (malaria!) laid me low there; Sarah Kline, Roz Hunt, and the team at Malaria No More (UK), who couldn't have set up more interviews and who answered every request with speed and entrepreneurialism; and Emily Bergantino at Malaria No More (US), another demon at arranging hard-to-get interviews and always on hand to assist. A special thank you as well to Dr. Matthew Emer, Martin, Lameck, and Jimmy Ogwal in Apac, Uganda, for receiving me so graciously and going out of their way to tell their stories.

Others who provided crucial help and support include Margaret Chan and Ian Smith at the World Health Organization; Rebecca Ladbury, who first introduced me to the fascinating world of malaria; Tachi Yamada, Gabrielle Fitzgerald, Deborah Lacy, Laurie Lee, and Katie Harris at the Bill & Melinda Gates Foundation; Peter Chernin; Richard Curtis; Simon Fuller; Andy Murray, Julian Henry, and Matthew Gentry; Brian Greenwood; Bob Snow and Lydia Mwangi in Nairobi; Christina Barrineau and John Allen; Yvonne Chaka Chaka and Louis da Gama; Margaret Bergen and all at the Center for Interfaith Action; Lindsay Crouse, Victor Zonana, and Daniel Gwinnell at Global Health Strategies; John Bridgeland, who allowed me to travel with him through Rwanda and threw me an impromptu party in Kibuye for my thirty-ninth birthday; Marcel Tanner; Salim Abdullah and Gerry Killeen at the Ifakara malaria research station; Kate Roberts, Anna Dirksen, Trey Watkins, and Regina Moore at PSI; Admiral Tim Ziemer and Chris Thomas at the President's Malaria Initiative; Richard Feachem; Tim Wells and Jaya Banerji at Medicines for Malaria Venture; Christian Loucq, Alexandra Fullem, and David A. Poland at the PATH Malaria Vaccine Initiative; Janet Hemingway; Peter Mullen; Carol Lin Vieira at Burness Communications; Sarah Staedke and Heidi Hopkins in Jinja, Uganda; Allison Branham and Erika Arthun at Williamsworks; the president of Rwanda, Paul Kagame; Joe Cohen and Stephen Rea at GlaxoSmithKline; Ed Scott; Scott Case; Mark Green; Carol Hooks at the World Bank; Tony Blair, Ian Linden, Hannah Wallace, Parna Taylor, and Susie McShane at the Tony Blair Faith Foundation, who provided the introduction to Michael Dwyer and Hurst Publishing; Rob Young at ExxonMobil; Jennifer Gregoire at the Clinton Health Access Initiative; Josh Ruxin; Parag Khanna; Ghanian health minister George Sipa-Adja

Yankey; and Martin Dawes and Gaelle Bausson at UNICEF. Not all of these individuals or their organizations are mentioned in the book, but all of them contributed immensely to my understanding of malaria and the campaign.

I was extremely lucky to be able to call upon a host of friends, colleagues, and malaria experts, who all gave up days of their time to read through various drafts of the manuscript and make comments and corrections. Without exception, these were invaluable. Simon Robinson, a former colleague and editor at *Time*, and someone who shares my experience of Africa and India, went through the text with his usual meticulousness and offered wise and very specific advice on nuance, structure, and logic. Richard Brown went through the book line by line and offered great insight into structure and argument. Max Askew had wise words on narrative and composition and picked up a number of mistakes. Julian Marshall cast his expert eye over the financial sections and brought his eagle-eyed editing skills to bear on a late draft. Colin Perry was also a great help on the sections on business. Any remaining errors are my own.

Thanks also to Pieter Hugo, photographer supreme and friend, for gracefully agreeing to take the author picture and a special mention too to Dominic Nahr, star of Magnum and regular traveling companion, who agreed to let me use his pictures of Apac in some editions.

And finally, thanks and love to Tess, who reads all my drafts, and my girls, Katya, Grace, and now Olivia. Malaria kills children. Mine are why I wrote this.

Notes

CHAPTER 1

1. Paul Edward Okello, Win van Bortel, Anatol Maranda Byaruhanga, Anne Correwyn, Patricia Roelants, Ambrose Talisuna, Umberto d'Alessandro, and Marc Coosemans, "Variation in Malaria Transmission Intensity in Seven Sites Throughout Uganda," *American Journal of Tropical Medicine and Hygiene* 75, no. 2 (2006): 219–225, http://www.ajtmh.org/cgi/content/full/75/2/219.

2. Ibid.

3. Interview with Dr. Matthew Emer, Apac, August 2009. All quotations from Emer in this chapter are from this interview.

4. Interview with Lameck Abongo, Apac, August 2009. All quotations from Abongo in this chapter are from this interview.

CHAPTER 2

1. Brian M. Greenwood, David A. Fidock, Dennis E. Kyle, Stefan H. I. Kappe, Pedro L. Alonso, Frank H. Collins, and Patrick E. Duffy "Malaria: Progress, Perils, and Prospects for Eradication," *Journal of Clinical Investigation* 118, no. 4 (April 1, 2008): 1266–1276, http://www.ncbi.nlm.nih.gov/pmc/articles/PMC2276780/?tool=pmcentrez.

2. Mats Wahlgren and Maria Teresa Bejarano, "Malaria: A Blueprint of 'Bad Air,'" *Nature* 400 (Aug. 5, 1999): 506–507.

3. David L. Smith, F. Ellis McKenzie, Robert W. Snow, and Simon I. Hay, "Revisiting the Basic Reproductive Number for Malaria and Its Implications for Malaria Control," Hay, *Public Library of Science: Biology*, Feb. 20, 2007, http://www.plosbiology.org/article/info:doi/10.1371/journal.pbio.0050042.

4. Emma Rabino Massa, Nicoletta Cerutti, and A. Marin D. Savoia, "Malaria in Ancient Egypt: Paleoimmunological Investigation on Predynastic Mummified Remains," *Chungara: Revista de Antropología Chilena* 32, no. 1 (2000): 7–9, http://www.scielo.cl/scielo.php?pid=S0717-73562000000100003&script=sci_arttext.

5. Sonia Shah, *The Fever: How Malaria Has Ruled Humankind for 500,000 Years* (New York: Sarah Chrichton Books/Farrar, Straus, and Giroux, 2010). Of all the histories of malaria and malariology, Shah's has the dual virtue of being the most comprehensive survey of malaria literature and the most recent.

6. Brian Greenwood, "Malaria Chemoprophylaxis in Endemic Regions," in *Malaria: Waiting for the Vaccine*, ed. G. A. T. Targett, London School of Hygiene and Tropical Medicine First Annual Public Health Forum (New York: John Wiley and Sons, 1991), 83.

7. John Noble Wilford, "Malaria Is a Likely Killer in King Tut's Post-Mortem," *New York Times*, Feb. 16, 2010, http://www.nytimes.com/2010/02/17/science/17tut.html.

8. Shah, *The Fever*, 91.

9. "Frequently Asked Questions," The Resource to the Sickle Cell Disease Patient, http://sicklecell.md/faq.asp#q9.

10. Cheston B. Cunha and Burke A. Cunha, "Brief History of the Clinical Diagnosis of Malaria: From Hippocrates to Osler," *Journal of Vector Borne Diseases* 45 (Sept. 2008): 194–199, http://www.mrcindia.org/journal/issues/453194.pdf.

11. Fiammetta Rocco, *The Miraculous Fever Tree: Malaria and the Quest for a Cure that Changed the World* (New York: HarperCollins, 2003).

12. Telephone interview with Richard Feachem, April 2009.

13. Shah, *The Fever*, 182–184.

14. Ibid., 189–190.

15. http://www.ibiblio.org/hyperwar/USA/ref/Ann/index.html.

16. Shah, *The Fever*, 194–196.

17. Ibid., 207.

18. Ibid., 199.

19. David Cutler, Winnie Fung, Michael Kremer, and Monica Singhal, "Mosquitoes: The Long-Term Effects of Malaria Eradication in India," Harvard University, May 2007, http://www.hks.harvard.edu/var/ezp_site/storage/fckeditor/file/pdfs/centers-programs/centers/cid/growth/events/20070531/gates_cutler_malaria_070527.pdf.

20. Shah, *The Fever*, 199.

21. Ibid., 212–216.

22. Patrick T. O'Shaughnessy, "The Flying Cat Story, or 'Operation Cat Drop': A History of This Often-Told Tale," n.d., http://cat drop.com.

23. Shah, *The Fever* 211.

24. Ibid., 205.

25. Telephone interview with Feachem, April 2009.

26. Ibid., 216.

27. Interview with Brian Greenwood, Nairobi, November 2009. All quotations from Greenwood in this chapter are from this interview.

28. Interview with Marcel Tanner, Ifakara Health Institute, Tanzania, August 2009.

29. Interview with Bob Snow, Nairobi, May 2009.

30. P. L. Alonso, S. W. Lindsay, J. R. Armstrong, M. Conteh, A. G. Hill, P. H. David, G. Fegan, A. de Francisco, A. J. Hall, F. T. Shenton, et al., "The Effect of Insecticide-Treated Bed Nets on Mortality of Gambian Children," *Lancet*, 337 (June 22, 1991): 1499–1502, http://www.ncbi.nlm.nih.gov/pubmed/1675368.

31. Interview with Christian Lengeler, Basel, June 2009. All quotations from Lengeler in this chapter are from this interview.

CHAPTER 3

1. Interview with Ray Chambers en route from Tanzania to Uganda, August 2009.

2. Ford S. Worthy, "Wes Threatens to Pull Out of Wesray," *Fortune*, July 21, 1986, http://money.cnn.com/magazines/fortune/fortune_archive/1986/07/21/67874/index.htm; Leslie Brody, Alan Farnham, David Kirkpatrick, Christopher Knowlton, and Patricia Sellers, "Sans Simon, Wesray Cleans Up on Avis," *Fortune*, October 26, 1987, http://money.cnn.com/magazines/fortune/fortune_archive/1987/10/26/69748/index.htm.

3. Ralph T. King Jr., "Ray of Hope: A Modest Millionaire Quits Business to Help Rebuild Newark, N.J.," *Wall Street Journal*, Sept. 30, 1992, A1, http://cim.ou.edu/kingralph.htm.

4. Telephone interview with Suprotik Basu, October 2010. All quotations from Basu in this chapter are from this interview.

5. David D. Kirkpatrick, "Hoop Springs Eternal," *New York Magazine*, Feb. 15, 1999, http://nymag.com/nymetro/news/sports/features/993/index3.html

6. Telephone interview with Steven Phillips, November 2010. All quotations from Phillips in this chapter are from this interview.

7. See Alex Perry, *Falling Off the Edge: Travels Through the Dark Heart of Globalization* (London: Macmillan; New York: Bloomsbury, 2008), where these arguments are explored in full.

8. See United Nations Development Programme, "What Are the Millennium Development Goals?" n.d., http://www.undp.org/mdg/basics.shtml.

9. John Luke Gallup and Jeffrey D. Sachs, "The Economic Burden of Malaria," CID Working Paper No. 52, Center for International Development, Harvard University, July 2000, http://www.hks.harvard.edu/centers/cid/publications/faculty-working-papers/cid-working-paper-no.-52.

CHAPTER 4

1. "Global Recession Threatens Human Rights of Poorest, Warns UN Rights Chief," UN News Centre, Feb. 20, 2009, http://www.un.org/apps/news/story.asp?NewsID=29962&Cr=financial+crisis&Cr1.

2. World Bank, "Global Crisis Prompts Big Rise in World Bank Health and Education Financing: AIDS Drugs Could Be in Short Supply," News Release 2009/324/HDN, April 24, 2009, http://web.world

bank.org/wbsite/external/topics/exteducation/0,,contentmdk:2215
5700~menuPK:282423~pagePK:64020865~piPK:149114~theSitePK:28
2386,00.html.

3. "Development Committee Press Conference, Remarks by World
Bank President Robert B. Zoellick," World Bank News and Broadcast, April 26, 2009, http://web.worldbank.org/wbsite/external/news/
0,,contentMDK:22157110~pagePK:64257043~piPK:437376~theSite
PK:4607,00.html.

4. Dominique Strauss-Kahn, "Changes: Successful Partnerships for
Africa's Growth Challenge," Dar es Salaam, Tanzania, March 10,
2009, http://www.imf.org/external/np/speeches/2009/031009.htm.

5. Jeremy Clift, "Africa Faces Twin Challenges After Global Crisis,"
IMF Survey Magazine, March 4, 2010, http://www.imf.org/external/
pubs/ft/survey/so/2010/NEW030410A.htm.

6. "IMF Trims Sub-Saharan Africa's 2011 Growth Forecast," Reuters,
Oct. 6, 2010, http://af.reuters.com/article/topNews/idAFJOE6950F42
0101006; "Development Aid Rose in 2009 and Most Donors Will
Meet 2010 Aid Targets," OECD, April 14, 2010, http://www.oecd.org/
document/11/0,3343,en_2649_34487_44981579_1_1_1_1,00.html.

7. "Africa Sustains Social Spending Despite Downturn," IMF Survey
Magazine, April 23, 2010, http://www.imf.org/external/pubs/ft/survey/
so/2010/CAR042310B.htm.

8. "Transcript of a Press Briefing on the IMF's Economic Outlook
for Sub-Saharan Africa," Washington, DC, April 23, 2010, http://
www.imf.org/external/np/tr/2010/tr042310.htm.

9. Regional Economic Outlook, Sub-Saharan Africa, April 2009,
http://www.imf.org/external/pubs/ft/reo/2009/afr/eng/sreo0409.pdf.

10. Jim Lobe and Eli Clifton, "World Bank, NGOs Exhort G20 Not
to Forget the Poorest," Inter Press Service, Sept. 16, 2009, http://ipsnews
.net/news.asp?idnews=48465.

11. Ibid.

12. Ibid.

13. William Easterly, "The Cartel of Good Intentions: Bureaucracy
Versus Markets in Foreign Aid" (Working Paper 4, Center for Global
Development, March 2002), 42.

14. Shaohua Chen and Martin Ravallion, "How Have the World's Poorest Fared Since the Early 1980s?" (World Bank Policy Research Working Paper 3341, Development Research Group, World Bank, June 2004), http://www-wds.worldbank.org/external/default/WDSContentServer/WDSP/IB/2004/07/22/000112742_20040722172047/Rendered/PDF/wps3341.pdf.

15. Bate Felix, "Global Aid Rose in 2009 but Missed Target: OECD," Reuters, April 14, 2010, http://af.reuters.com/article/topNews/idAFJOE63D0LL20100414.

16. Alex Perry, "The Cost of Giving," *Time* (European edition; cover), Aug. 18, 2008, http://www.time.com/time/magazine/article/0,9171,1830201,00.html. See also Alex Perry, "Ethiopia: Pain amid Plenty," *Time*, Aug. 6, 2008, http://www.time.com/time/magazine/article/0,9171,1829841,00.html; and Alex Perry, "Among the Starving in Ethiopia," *Time*, Aug. 6, 2008, http://www.time.com/time/world/article/0,8599,1829996,00.html.

17. "Global Targets, Local Ingenuity," *Economist*, Sept. 23, 2010, www.economist.com/node/17090934.

18. Ibid.; Maureen Lewis, "Governance and Corruption in Public Health Care Systems" (Working Paper Number 78, Center for Global Development, January 2006), http://www.usaid.gov/our_work/democracy_and_governance/technical_areas/anticorruption_handbook/annexes/subannexes/Health/Health1%20-%20Lewis%20-%202006.pdf.

19. Michael Sheridan, "Massive Fraud Hits Tsunami Aid," *Times* (London), April 16, 2006, http://www.timesonline.co.uk/tol/news/world/article706115.ece.

20. "Salaries and Post Adjustment," United Nations, 2003–2011, http://www.un.org/Depts/OHRM/salaries_allowances/salary.htm.

21. Imogen Foulkes, "UN Warns of Refugee Camp Dangers to Children," BBC News, Sept. 15, 2010, http://www.bbc.co.uk/news/world-europe-11307679.

22. "21st Century Aid: Recognizing Success and Tackling Failure" (Briefing Paper 137, Oxfam, April 28, 2010), http://www.oxfam.org/sites/www.oxfam.org/files/bp137–21st-century-aid-summary.pdf.

23. Nick Wadhams, "Bad Charity? (All I Got Was This Lousy T-Shirt)" *Time*, May 12, 2010, http://www.time.com/time/world/article/0,8599,1987628,00.html.

CHAPTER 5

1. "Population," Lagos State Government, 2011, http://www.lagosstate.gov.ng/index.php?page=subpage&spid=12&mnu=null.

2. "International Energy Statistics: Petroleum," Independent Statistics and Analysis, US Energy Information Administration, n.d., http://tonto.eia.doe.gov/cfapps/ipdbproject/IEDIndex3.cfm?tid=5&pid=53&aid=1.

3. "Diamond Facts: Fact 9: Approximately $8.5 Billion Worth of Diamonds a Year Come from African Countries," The World Diamond Council, n.d., http://www.diamondfacts.org/facts/fact_09.html.

4. Interview with Steven Phillips, Rwanda, June 2009. All quotations from Phillips in this chapter are from this interview.

5. The 92-meter, $100 million *Tatoosh* and the 127-meter, $200 million *Octopus*, which carries two helicopters, seven boats, two submarines, a swimming pool, a music studio, a basketball court, and sixty crew.

6. Interview with Steven Knowles, Accra, December 2009. All quotations from Knowles in this chapter are from this interview.

7. "Background and Objectives of LSDI Malaria Control Programme in Maputo Province," Lubombo Spatial Development Initiative, http://www.malaria.org.za/lsdi/Background/BackgroundMaputo/background.html.

8. The company was renamed after Anglo American consolidated its gold mining interests in 1998.

9. Steven Knowles, "Malaria Control as a Best Practice Corporate Social Responsibility Programme," AngloGold Ashanti, 3, http://www.afmeurope.org/IMG/pdf/6.SteveKnowles_Paris_presentation_GF.pdf.

10. Telephone interview with Ray Chambers, October 2010.

CHAPTER 6

1. Telephone interview with Christian Lengeler, June 2009. All quotations from Lengeler in this chapter are from this interview.

2. "Doctors Welcome Malaria Microchip," BBC, April 24, 2009, http://news.bbc.co.uk/2/hi/uk_news/scotland/glasgow_and_west/8015241.stm.

3. FeiFei Jiang, "No Love for Mosquitoes," *IAEA Bulletin* 50, no. 1 (2008), http://www.iaea.org/Publications/Magazines/Bulletin/Bull501/SIT.html.

4. "Sex Intervention Combats Malaria," BBC, Dec. 22, 2009, http://news.bbc.co.uk/2/hi/health/8426798.stm.

5. Interview with Brian Greenwood, Nairobi, November 2009.

6. Telephone interview with anonymous expert, November 2010.

7. Telephone interview with member of White House staff, November 2010.

8. PEPFAR's funding was expanded to $48 billion in 2008.

9. White House Archives, "President Discusses G8 Summit, Progress in Africa," June 30, 2005, http://georgewbush-whitehouse.archives.gov/news/releases/2005/06/20050630.html.

10. Telephone interview with malaria expert, November 2010.

11. Telephone interview with Suprotik Basu, October 2010.

12. Telephone interview with Ray Chambers, November 2010.

13. All quotations from the summit are from "White House Summit on Malaria: A World Where Malaria Is No More," Kaiser Network, Dec. 14, 2006.

14. Interview with Gabrielle Fitzgerald, Zanzibar, Tanzania, August 2009. All quotations from Fitzgerald in this chapter are from this interview.

15. Email interview with Richard Curtis, March 2007.

16. Email interview with Simon Fuller, November 2010.

17. Matt, "American Idol: Idol Gives Back Results Show Recap—April 25, 2007," Wild Bluff Media, April 25, 2007, http://www.wildbluffmedia.com/2007/04/25/american-idol-idol-gives-back-results-show-recap.

18. "Bill and Melinda Gates Call for New Global Commitment to Chart a Course for Malaria Eradication," press release, Bill & Melinda Gates Foundation, Oct. 17, 2007, http://www.gatesfoundation.org/press-releases/Pages/course-for-malaria-eradication-071017–2.aspx.

CHAPTER 7

1. Interview with Margaret Chan, Kampala, Uganda, August 2009.
2. Telephone interview with Ray Chambers, November 2010. All quotations from Chambers in this chapter are from this interview.
3. Telephone interview with Suprotik Basu, October 2010. All quotations from Basu in this chapter are from this interview.
4. "'Idol Gives Back' Raises Almost $45 Million for Charity," Reuters, April 23, 2010, http://www.reuters.com/article/idUSTRE63L0BV20100423.
5. Ban Ki-Moon, "Let's Get to Work," *Guardian*, April 25, 2008, http://www.guardian.co.uk/commentisfree/2008/apr/25/letsgettowork.
6. Telephone interview with Alan Court, October 2010. All quotations from Court in this chapter are from this interview.
7. Perhaps not altogether surprising. They are produced by drug companies whose business is selling pills.
8. "White House Summit on Malaria: A World Where Malaria Is No More," Kaiser Network, Dec. 14, 2006, http://www.kaisernetwork.org/health_cast/uploaded_files/121406_whitehouse_malaria_transcript.pdf.
9. "2008 MDG Malaria Summit: World Leaders Commit Record Billions to Tackle Malaria," Transcript, Office of the UN Secretary-General's Special Envoy for Malaria, Sept. 25, 2008, http://malariaenvoy.com/MDGSummit/tabid/83/Default.aspx.

CHAPTER 8

1. Telephone interview with Richard Feachem, April 2009.
2. Telephone interview with Scott Case, December 2009.

3. In 2010, the figure would be revised again, to 765 million.

4. Alex Mwita, speaking at a roundtable meeting with Tanzanian health professionals and Chambers, Chan, and Yamada, Amana District Hospital, Dar es Salaam, August 2009.

5. Ray Chambers, meeting, Amana District Hospital, August 2009.

6. Interview with Chambers in Dar es Salaam, August 2009.

7. Excerpt from my notes, meeting, Amana District Hospital, August 2009.

8. Interview with Alan Court, Dar es Salaam, August 2009.

9. A fifth would be turned down in November 2009.

10. Interview with Court, August 2009.

11. Press conference at Entebbe International Airport, August 19, 2009.

12. Chan, meeting at the Uganda National Malaria Control Program offices in Kampala, August 20, 2009.

13. Conversation with Chambers and Court at Bulima, Uganda, August 20, 2009.

14. Roundtable meeting with Quality Chemical Industries and Chambers, Chan, and Yamada, Kampala, August 20, 2009.

15. Conversation with Chambers, Kampala, August 2009.

CHAPTER 9

1. Interviews with Laura Hoemeke, senior development worker, and Eric Munyemana, Kigali, June 2009.

2. Rick Warren, sermon, Saddleback Church, August 2008, http://www.christianpost.com/news/the-seven-pillars-that-make-peace-34006.

3. Interview with Blaise Karibushi, Kigali, June 2009.

4. Interview with Antoine Rutayisire, Kigali, June 2009.

5. Remarks by Dr. Lennie Bazira Kyomuhangi, meeting with Saddleback Church members, Kibuye, June 2009.

6. Warren, sermon, August 2008.

7. Interview with Eric Munyemana, Kibuye, June 2009.

8. Interview with Ray Chambers, Abuja, December 2009.

9. Interview with Tom Woods, Abuja, December 2009. All quotations from Woods in this chapter are from this interview.

10. Remarks by Woods and Onno Rühl, Abuja's Central Mosque, December 2009.

11. Interview with Chambers, Abuja, December 2009.

12. Interview with Alhaji Muhammad Sa'ad Abubakar, Abuja, December 2009

13. Remarks by Chambers, roundtable breakfast meeting with Nigeria's malaria community, Abuja, December 2009.

CHAPTER 10

1. All quotations from Suprotik Basu in this chapter are from conversations during our trip to and travels in Kenya, December 2009.

2. All quotations in this section are from the meeting at the Kenyan Health Ministry, Nairobi, December 2009.

CHAPTER 11

1. Interview with Marcel Tanner, Ifakara Health Institute, Tanzania, August 2009. All quotations from Tanner in this chapter are from this interview.

2. Telephone interview with Alan Court, December 2010. All quotations from Court in this chapter are from this interview.

3. Telephone interview with Suprotik Basu, December 2010. All quotations from Basu in this chapter are from this interview.

4. Telephone interview with Patrick Mullen, December 2010. All quotations from Mullen in this chapter are from this interview.

5. Interview with Dr. Benjamin Atua Matindii, Kinshasa, June 2009.

CHAPTER 12

1. Interview with Marcel Tanner, Ifakara Health Institute, Tanzania, August 2009.

2. Andy Murray, email communication with the author, October 1, 2010.

3. Telephone interviews with Sarah Kline, October 2010 and January 2011. All quotations from Kline in this chapter are from these interviews.

4. Alan Court, email communication with the author, February 2011.

5. Interview with Ray Chambers, August 2009.

CHAPTER 13

1. Interviews with Brian Greenwood, Nairobi, December 2009.

2. Interview with Marcel Tanner, Ifakara Health Institute, August 2009.

3. Telephone interview with Suprotik Basu, October 2010. All quotations from Basu in this chapter are from this interview.

4. *Regional Economic Outlook: Sub-Saharan Africa: Resilience and Risks* (Washington, DC: International Monetary Fund, 2010), 1, http://www.imf.org/external/pubs/ft/reo/2010/AFR/eng/pdf/sreo1010 .pdf.

5. *Regional Economic Outlook: Sub-Saharan Africa* (Washington, DC: International Monetary Fund, 2008), 27.

6. Paul Collier and Witney Schneidman, "Sustaining Growth Will Challenge Govts," allAfrica.com, Feb. 20, 2009, http://allafrica.com/ stories/200902200088.html.

7. Telephone interview with Stephen Hayes, February 2009.

8. Telephone interview with Dambisa Moyo, February 2009.

9. Interview with Mulugeta Aserate Kassa, Addis Ababa, August 2007.

10. Telephone interview with Andrew Rugasira, February 2009.

11. A series of studies by, variously, the London Business School, the World Bank, and the consultant Deloitte's found that for every extra ten mobile phones per hundred people in a developing country, GDP rose 0.6–1.2 percent. Phones that offered mobile banking would be expected to raise that further, though studies are yet to be carried out.

12. "Coping with Today's Global Challenges in the Context of the Strategy of the United Nations Convention to Combat Desertification," High Level Dialogue, UNCCD, May 27, 2008, http://www.cn5195 .com/english/Page.asp?Language=Gb2312&ID=3131.

13. Telephone interview with Chris Reij, April 2009. All quotations from Reij in this chapter are from this interview.

14. Telephone interview with Ray Chambers, November 2010. All quotations from Chambers in this chapter are from this interview.

15. According to Basu, interview, October 2010.

CHAPTER 14

1. World Health Organization, "Summary," in *World Malaria Report 2010*, xv, http://www.who.int/malaria/world_malaria_report _2010/en/.

2. Ibid., xi.

3. *Regional Economic Outlook: Sub-Saharan Africa: Resilience and Risks* (Washington, DC: International Monetary Fund, 2010), 72, http://www.imf.org/external/pubs/ft/reo/2010/AFR/eng/pdf/sreo1010.pdf.

4. Telephone interview with Tony Blair, February 2009.

5. Interview with Margaret Chan, Kampala, Uganda, August 2009.

6. "Remarks by Dr. Rajiv Shah," Center for Global Development, USAID, Washington, DC, Jan. 19, 2011, http://www.usaid.gov/press/ speeches/2011/sp110119.html.

7. Daniel Martin, "Britain Cuts Aid to China and Russia After Inquiry Rules They Are No Longer Poor . . . but We're Still Giving India £280m," *Daily Mail*, Feb. 28, 2011, http://www.dailymail.co.uk/ news/article-1361165/Britain-cuts-aid-China-Russia-giving-India -280m.html.

8. Gabrielle Fitzgerald at the Gates Foundation called the Methodist move "a revival. Before they had missionaries across Africa. Now they're rededicating their church to rediscovering their roots, and the founding principles of John Wesley, and they have a seat at the table at the Global Fund" (interview with Gabrielle Fitzgerald, Zanzibar, Tanzania, August 2009).

9. Giving USA Foundation, "How a Recession Impacts Giving," *Netlinks*, special edition, June 2008, http://www.ruotoloassoc.com/newsletter/SpecialEditionJune08.pdf; Ret Boney, "US Giving Hits Record $306 Billion," *Philanthropy Journal*, June 23, 2008, http://www.philanthropyjournal.org/news/us-giving-hits-record-306-billion.

10. *The Index of Global Philanthropy and Remittances 2010* (Washington, DC: Hudson Institute, 2010), 13, http://www.hudson.org/files/pdf_upload/Index_of_Global_Philanthropy_and_Remittances_2010.pdf.

11. AP Enterprise, "Fraud Plagues Global Health Fund," Associated Press, Jan. 24, 2011, http://www.google.com/hostednews/ap/article/ALeqM5jBNgIu-Vg-_pAVtF6PcN9eSYPfiA?docId=eccd6da0cec34b489a67dfdf80cb933b; Andrew Jack, "UN Health Fund to Review Practices," *Financial Times* (London), Feb. 3, 2011, http://www.ft.com/cms/s/0/bd2d513a-2fcd-11e0–91f8–00144feabdc0.html#axzz1DUQkzgcf; "Foundation Support for the Global Fund," Bill & Melinda Gates Foundation, Jan. 24. 2011, http://www.gatesfoundation.org/press-releases/pages/support-for-the-global-fund-110124.aspx.

12. World Health Organization, "Summary," in *World Malaria Report 2010*, xi.

13. Ibid.

14. Telephone interview with Suprotik Basu, January 2011. All quotations from Basu in this chapter are from this interview.

15. Telephone interview with Alan Court, December 2011.

16. Telephone interview with Steven Phillips, November 2010.

17. Telephone interview with Peter Chernin, December 2009. All quotations from Chernin in this chapter are from this interview.

18. Telephone interview with Tachi Yamada, December 2010.

19. Telephone interview with Christian Lengeler, June 2009.

20. Patrick Worsnip and Kate Kelland, "Global Fund Sees Disease Fight Hampered by Donors," Reuters, Oct. 5, 2010, http://www.reuters.com/article/idUSTRE6945JE20101005.

21. Ania Lichtarowicz, "Malaria Funding 'Falling Short,'" BBC News, Oct. 1, 2010, http://www.bbc.co.uk/news/health-11453519.

22. Telephone interview with Richard Feachem, April 2009.

23. Interview with Marcel Tanner, Ifakara Health Institute, Tanzania, August 2009.

24. Sonia Shah, "Live with It," *Le Monde Diplomatique*, Oct. 2010, 1, http://mondediplo.com/2010/10/13malaria.

25. "Malaria Elimination," *Lancet*, Oct. 29, 2010, http://www.the lancet.com/malaria-elimination.

26. Telephone interview with Ian Linden, February 2010.

27. Jeffrey Sachs, "Aid Ironies," *Huffington Post*, May 24, 2009, http://www.huffingtonpost.com/jeffrey-sachs/aid-ironies_b_207181 .html.

28. William Easterly, "Sachs Ironies: Why Critics Are Better for Foreign Aid Than Apologists," *Huffington Post*, May 25, 2009, http://www.huffingtonpost.com/william-easterly/sachs-ironies-why-critics _b_207331.html.

29. Dambisa Moyo, "Aid Ironies: A Response to Jeffrey Sachs," *Huffington Post*, May 26, 2009, http://www.huffingtonpost.com/ dambisa-moyo/aid-ironies-a-response-to_b_207772.html.

30. Jeffrey Sachs and John W. McArthur, "Moyo's Confused Attack on Aid for Africa," *Huffington Post*, May 27, 2009, http://www.huffington post.com/jeffrey-sachs/moyos-confused-attack-on_b_208222.html.

31. World Health Organization, *World Malaria Report 2010*; World Health Organization, *World Malaria Report 2009*, http://www.who .int/malaria/world_malaria_report_2009/en/index.html.

32. When Chambers started on Apr. 25, 2008, he already had 130 million nets in hand: 99 million from the Global Fund and the World Bank, 20 million from the UK, and 10 million from the US. Between then and the halfway mark, August 2009, he pushed the total to 182 million; by year's end 2010, it was 289 million.

33. Roll Back Malaria, "Saving Lives with Malaria Control: Counting Down to the Millennium Development Goals," *Progress and Impact Series*, no. 3 (September 2010): 25, http://www.rbm.who.int/ ProgressImpactSeries/docs/report3-en.pdf.

34. Telephone interview with Christian Lengeler, January 2011.

Index

Alex Perry is *Time*'s Africa bureau chief, covering forty-eight countries in sub-Saharan Africa. From 2002 to 2006, he was South Asia bureau chief, based in New Delhi, covering Afghanistan to Bangladesh. He joined *Time* as a staff writer and travel editor in Hong Kong in February 2001. His journalism has won numerous awards. His twenty *Time* cover stories have ranged from Afghanistan, Iraq, the Asian tsunami, and the Kashmir quake to hunger in Ethiopia, South Africa's 2009 elections, South Africa's 2010 World Cup, Zimbabwe, the illegal Africa-to-Asia trade in rhino horn, Asia's child slave trade, and Bangladesh's emergence from terror and poverty. He is the author of *Falling Off the Edge: Globalization, World Peace and Other Lies* (2009). He lives in Cape Town with his wife and three daughters.

PublicAffairs is a publishing house founded in 1997. It is a tribute to the standards, values, and flair of three persons who have served as mentors to countless reporters, writers, editors, and book people of all kinds, including me.

I.F. STONE, proprietor of *I. F. Stone's Weekly*, combined a commitment to the First Amendment with entrepreneurial zeal and reporting skill and became one of the great independent journalists in American history. At the age of eighty, Izzy published *The Trial of Socrates*, which was a national bestseller. He wrote the book after he taught himself ancient Greek.

BENJAMIN C. BRADLEE was for nearly thirty years the charismatic editorial leader of *The Washington Post*. It was Ben who gave the *Post* the range and courage to pursue such historic issues as Watergate. He supported his reporters with a tenacity that made them fearless and it is no accident that so many became authors of influential, best-selling books.

ROBERT L. BERNSTEIN, the chief executive of Random House for more than a quarter century, guided one of the nation's premier publishing houses. Bob was personally responsible for many books of political dissent and argument that challenged tyranny around the globe. He is also the founder and longtime chair of Human Rights Watch, one of the most respected human rights organizations in the world.

·   ·   ·

For fifty years, the banner of Public Affairs Press was carried by its owner Morris B. Schnapper, who published Gandhi, Nasser, Toynbee, Truman, and about 1,500 other authors. In 1983, Schnapper was described by *The Washington Post* as "a redoubtable gadfly." His legacy will endure in the books to come.

Peter Osnos, *Founder and Editor-at-Large*